DEAD DAISIES MAKE ME CRAZY

OTHER BOOKS BY
LOREN NANCARROW AND JANET HOGAN TAYLOR

Dead Snails Leave No Trails
(Ten Speed Press, 1996)

The Worm Book
(Ten Speed Press, 1998)

DEAD DAISIES
MAKE
ME CRAZY

Garden Solutions without Chemical Pollution

LOREN NANCARROW
and JANET HOGAN TAYLOR

TEN SPEED PRESS
Berkeley   Toronto

A Kirsty Melville Book

Ten Speed Press
PO Box 7123
Berkeley, California 94707
www.tenspeed.com

Distributed in Australia by Simon and Schuster Australia, in Canada by Ten Speed Press Canada, in New Zealand by Southern Publishers Group, in South Africa by Real Books, and in the United Kingdom and Europe by Airlift Book Company.

Cover and Text Design by Libby Oda
Cover Illustrations by Ellen Sasaki
Interior Illustrations by Janet Hogan Taylor

Library of Congress Cataloging-in-Publication Data

Nancarrow, Loren.
    Dead daisies make me crazy : garden solutions without chemical pollution / Loren Nancarrow and Janet Hogan Taylor.
        p.   cm.
    Includes bibliographical references (pp. 165–67).
    ISBN-10: 1-58008-156-8 (pbk.)
    ISBN-13: 978-158008-156-6 (pbk.)
    1. Garden pests—Biological control. 2. Plant diseases.
3. Plants, Protection of. 4. Organic gardening. I. Taylor, Janet Hogan, 1954-   II. Title

SB974.N36   2000
635'.04996—dc21   99-089595

First printing, 2000
Printed in the United States of America

6 7 8 9 — 09 08 07 06 05

CONTENTS

Chapter 4: Make-It-Yourself Fertilizers, Mulches, and Compost 75

Chapter 5: Planting, Potting, and Maintenance Solutions, and Some Tips on Tools ...101

Chapter 6: Wildlife Loves an Organic Garden 127

Acknowledgments

We wish to express our gratitude to the following people: Julie Castiglia, our agent and friend; Kirsty Melville, our publisher; our families—Susie, Graham, Hannah, and Britta; and Brian, Evan, Leah, and Sue—who managed to live with us while we wrote this book; organic gardeners everywhere, who know that this is the way to go; the television and radio audiences that have given us tips and field-tested our ideas; and finally, all of our friends who have encouraged us along the way.

Thank you all!

Introduction

On a cool December morning, I sat cross-legged on the ground beneath a small citrus tree and learned something wonderful about my daughters. Hannah and Britta are just like me. They love the simple pleasures that nature can bring if allowed into our lives. As we sat and peeled small, sweet mandarin oranges we watched our local pair of roadrunners poke around under the orchard mulch looking for grubs. The girls were in heaven. The late fall crop of oranges was as full of sugar as any fruit could possibly be, and as we enjoyed our breakfast, we were also reaping the rewards of opening our little farm to nature. Too often the act of growing plants for food and pleasure sets the gardener at odds with the natural world around us. It needn't be the case. As cities grow and natural wildlife habitat shrinks, the enlightened approach to growing must include places where wildlife can share ground with us. Places where they can find food and appropriate shelter can make our gardens pleasing to the eye and provide important elements in a wildlife network.

We invite you to read along as we share our methods for growing plants without the use of inorganic chemical pesticides and fertilizers. Allow us to share methods for making and using your own blend of organic fertilizers to build the soil, thus making healthier plants. We hope to show you how you can be your own plant doctor by recognizing and correcting nutrient deficiencies. There are many ways to combat plant problems besides reaching for the quick fix in a bottle.

As you read, you'll also begin to understand the habits of the beautiful butterfly sipping nectar from your flower garden. You'll understand the intricacies of the fence lizard doing pushups, and know why skunks dig little holes in your lawn. As a gardener, it's likely that you spend more time outside than most people do. We hope our experiences as naturalists and gardeners will help you appreciate and embrace the fascinating landscape you've created.

We live in a push-button world. We turn on our conveniences with a button, and too often we kill what bugs us with a simple spray. As organic gardeners we are still faced with pests that compete for our harvest.

But because we believe that chemical pollution has harmed our environment, we have come up with a variety of clever methods to deal with insect and animal pests while keeping the air, water, and ground around our homes poison-free. Ninety-five percent of all the bugs in your yard are good guys, there to help you. As you read this book we believe you'll be better empowered to understand the delicate relationship we have with nature. You'll learn to participate in nature without destroying this important balance. Gardening in an organic, chemical-free way, you'll give back to our environment that has given us so much.

— Loren Nancarrow

Why Organic?

When we talk about *organic* we are talking about a method of working with nature and natural products to improve the soil and the environment we live in. Artificially produced fertilizers and pesticides have been cited as the two major soil pollutants in this country. The point is to build soil health so that plants will become stronger and resistant to pests and diseases, and people won't have to apply more chemicals to control them.

The real problem now facing us is how to stop our dependency on synthetic substances. How do we find that balance in nature again?

OUR IMPACT ON THE FOOD SUPPLY

One of the issues we have to address is our food supply. Can we live with tiny blemishes on the produce we buy in order to have a healthier environment? The Environmental Working Group, an environmental research group based in Washington, D.C., compiled this list showing the produce on the marketplace today that has the most and least pesticide residues.

Least pesticide residue	Most pesticide residue
Avocados	Apples
Bananas	Apricots
Broccoli	Bell peppers
Brussels sprouts	Cantaloupe (Mexican grown)
Cauliflower	Celery
Corn	Cherries (U.S. grown)
Grapes (U.S. grown)	Cucumbers
Onions	Grapes (Chilean grown)
Plums	Peaches
Sweet potatoes	Spinach
Watermelon	Strawberries

In this country, the public's insistence on "perfect," unblemished produce and the economic necessity of high yields have trapped many farmers in the chemical cycle. But farmers are learning that synthetic fertilizers do nothing to benefit the soil in the long run. Many fertilizers actually do more harm than good by depositing excessive salts and contaminants in the soil. Pesticides used to stop crop-eating insects also destroy the microscopic organisms and earthworms in the soil that provide nutrients for the plants. And finally, all of these chemicals poured on the soil are leaching out into our drinking water for all of us to drink.

BUILDING GOOD SOIL

Thankfully, the damage done to our soil can be reversed. It may take some time, but it can be done. Soil has a balance, and knowing that balance and working to achieve it is the first step. We must understand that soil is a complex system of life, minerals, energy, and elements. Any one of these things out of balance damages our soil. When our soil is in balance and we mix it with sunlight and water, wonderful things can start to grow.

Most scientists agree that a balanced soil has approximately 25 percent air, 25 percent water, 45 percent minerals, and 5 percent humus and living organisms. It is biodiverse and contains insects, fungi, bacteria, earthworms, yeast, protozoa, algae, nematodes, and actinomycetes, to name a few. Many are microscopic—like bacteria, protozoa, and yeast—and are referred to as *microorganisms*. Those that are not microscopic—earthworms, for example—are referred to as *macroorganisms*.

The macroorganisms and microorganisms break down organic matter into basic elements that plants use for food. Many of them also are able to "fix" nitrogen—take it from the air and make it available to plants. The broken-down organic matter forms the humus component of the soil that holds and slowly releases minerals and nutrients to the plants. The other component of soil is made up of small rock particles that give soil its structure. Without the humus component, the structure component is sterile and unable to support plant life.

STEPS TO HEALTHY SOIL
IN YOUR GARDEN

When we work in our own gardens, our goal is to turn unhealthy soil that usually has a poor organic component, lacks air, and is chemically unbalanced into living soil that is in balance. To do this we must provide the basic nutrients and then let nature take its course.

DETERMINE JUST HOW OUT OF BALANCE THE SOIL IS BY HAVING IT TESTED

A soil test will tell you how much organic matter, minerals, and elements are in your soil. It will also test the pH and other chemical levels. After an initial soil test, it is often recommended that you have your soil retested each year and always take the sample from the same area. This way you can track your soil's progress and head off any problems early. If your yard or garden is large, it is also wise to do separate tests in each area. Label the samples carefully so you can trace each test back to the specific area. Soil sampling is becoming much more common, and many companies are now listed in local phone books. If you don't find a listing there, contact your local cooperative extension office for the one closest to your area, or check the buying guide at the back of this book for mail-in soil-testing companies.

A good balanced soil should look something like this:

Nutrient	Percentage of available nutrients or parts per million
Oxygen	4-5 percent
Humus	2.5-5.0 percent
Calcium	65-75 percent
Magnesium	12-20 percent
Potassium	3-7.5 percent
Phosphate	250-375 PPM
Sulfate	25-50 PPM
Nitrogen	20-40 PPM
Sodium	0.5-3.0 percent
Salt	400 PPM or less
Chlorides	80-120 PPM
Boron	0.8-2.0 PPM
Iron	200 PPM or more
Manganese	50-125 PPM
Copper	2-5 PPM
Zinc	10-20 PPM

GET SOME AIR INTO THE SOIL

Living organisms need oxygen. Hard and compacted soil has little room to allow air to penetrate. Turn the soil over with a turning fork or tiller to loosen it up.

ADD THE RIGHT FERTILIZERS

With the results of your soil test in hand, it's time to get the mineral content of the soil back in balance. Buy a good organic fertilizer like rock phosphate to achieve the correct mineral balance. Most nurseries and companies that sell organic fertilizer will be happy to recommend the correct fertilizer and application rate to correct your problem.

ADD ORGANIC MATTER TO THE SOIL

Now is also the time to feed the organisms living in your soil. The best way to do this is with compost. More organic matter stimulates the microorganisms and earthworms to produce more humus and nutrients for the soil. When they die, they in turn become food for the decaying process and other organisms. In the end the soil becomes rich with nutrients available to plants. Apply at least one inch of finished compost to good soil or three inches of partially composted material for very poor soil, and mix into the top six inches or so.

MULCH THE SOIL

In nature, leaf litter and plant debris are normally found around plants and on the soil. In time, this debris becomes food for earthworms and other organisms. It also holds moisture in the soil, prevents erosion, and shelters the soil from the drying effects of sun and wind. Place three to four inches of mulch on beds and around plants to protect the soil. To prevent rotting, be sure to keep the mulch about three to four inches away from the trunks of trees or plants.

DON'T USE INSECTICIDES OR PESTICIDES

These toxins only help to kill the microorganisms and macroorganisms you are trying to encourage. Good healthy plants that have received the proper nutrients from soil organisms can resist insect and disease attacks better than weakened and poorly nourished plants.

Building the soil and finding alternate methods of pest control are good first steps to a healthy environment. Even if that environment is only a small strip of ground next to a patio, or if it's acres of land, it all counts. As each piece of land starts growing healthy plants, it attracts wildlife looking for a place to live, eat, or reproduce. By gardening organically, we help keep the cycle of life going for the next generation.

Garden and Lawn
Diseases and Remedies

Gardening is often a rewarding experience, but when a previously beautiful plant, vegetable, tree, or lawn suddenly starts doing poorly, figuring out what the cause is can be frustrating. Certain diseases that commonly plague gardens and lawns are easily recognizable. Once you diagnose the problem, many nonchemical remedies are available for you to use.

GARDEN DISEASES, SYMPTOMS, AND CONTROLS

This list of common diseases for specific plants and trees will help you narrow down what is troubling yours. The most common problem, if known, is italicized. Following the list, many of the common diseases are discussed with information about how to prevent and control them. Some plant diseases have specialized names that correspond to the part of the plant that is affected. For example, wilt is caused by an organism that penetrates and affects the plant's water-conducting system. Crown gall is caused by an organism that stimulates abnormal growth at the plant's base. A blight is caused by an organism that kills the plant's tissue, and canker appears on the plant like open sores.

COMMON PLANT, VEGETABLE, AND TREE DISEASES

Flowers

ASTERS – Downy mildew, fusarium wilt, gray mold, mosaic viruses, powdery mildew, *rust*, and verticillium wilt

BEGONIAS – Damping off, gray mold, powdery mildew, and root rot

CALENDULAS – Fungal leaf spot, *mosaic viruses*, powdery mildew, and root and stem rot

CARNATIONS – Bacterial wilt, fusarium wilt, gray mold, rust, and southern blight

CHRYSANTHEMUMS – Crown gall, fusarium wilt, gray mold, mosaic viruses, powdery mildew, rust, southern blight, and verticillium wilt

COSMOS – *Bacterial canker*, fusarium wilt, mosaic viruses, powdery mildew, root rot, and rust

DAHLIAS – Crown gall, fusarium wilt, gray mold, mosaic viruses, powdery mildew, rust, and verticillium wilt

DELPHINIUMS – Bacterial canker, crown rot, mosaic viruses, and powdery mildew

GERANIUMS – Gray mold, mosaic viruses, oak root fungus, rust, and verticillium wilt

GLADIOLUS – Fusarium wilt, gray mold, mosaic viruses, root rot, and southern blight

HOLLYHOCKS – Anthracnose, powdery mildew, and rust

IMPATIENS – Damping off, fungal leaf spot, *root rot*, and southern blight

IRIS – Bacterial soft rot, botrytis blight, crown rot, *fungal leaf spot*, root rot, and rust

LILIES – Botrytis blight, chlorosis, fusarium wilt, gray mold, mosaic viruses, and southern blight

MARIGOLDS – Downy mildew, fusarium wilt, gray mold, mosaic viruses, southern blight, and verticillium wilt

NARCISSUS – Botrytis blight, fusarium wilt, leaf spot, and mosaic viruses

PANSIES – Downy mildew, powdery mildew, and southern blight

PEONIES – Botrytis blight, fusarium wilt, gray mold, and verticillium wilt

PETUNIAS – Botrytis blight, damping off, gray mold, mosaic viruses, powdery mildew, and verticillium wilt

PHLOX – Damping off, *powdery mildew*, root rot, and rust

POPPIES – Bacterial canker, botrytis blight, downy mildew, leaf spot, powdery mildew, and verticillium wilt

PRIMROSES – Gray mold

SNAPDRAGONS – Downy mildew, fusarium wilt, gray mold, mosaic viruses, powdery mildew, rust, and verticillium wilt

SWEET PEAS – Anthracnose, *bacterial canker*, mosaic viruses, powdery mildew, and root rot

TULIPS – Anthracnose, *botrytis blight*, fusarium wilt, mosaic viruses, powdery mildew, and southern blight

ZINNIAS – *Damping off*, gray mold, leaf spot, mosaic viruses, powdery mildew, and root rot

Fruit Trees, Bushes, and Vines

APPLES – Anthracnose, crown gall, fireblight, mosaic viruses, oak root fungus, powdery mildew, rust, scab, and southern blight

APRICOTS – Bacterial canker, *brown rot*, crown rot, gray mold, oak root fungus, powdery mildew, root rot, and shot hole fungus

BLACKBERRIES AND RASPBERRIES – Anthracnose, crown gall, downy mildew, gray mold, oak root fungus, powdery mildew, rust, and verticillium wilt

BLUEBERRIES – Gray mold, powdery mildew, and root rot

CHERRIES – *Bacterial canker*, brown rot of stone fruit, crown gall, gray mold, oak root fungus, powdery mildew, and root rot

CITRUS – Brown rot, root rot, and sooty mold

GRAPES – Anthracnose, crown gall, downy mildew, gray mold, oak root fungus, powdery mildew, root rot, and verticillium wilt

PEACHES AND NECTARINES – Brown rot of stone fruit, crown gall, mosaic viruses, oak root fungus, *peach tree curl*, powdery mildew, and shot hole fungus

PEARS – Bacterial canker, crown gall, fireblight, oak root fungus, rust, and scab

PLUMS AND PRUNES – Brown rot of stone fruit, crown gall, oak root fungus, powdery mildew, root rot, and rust

STRAWBERRIES – Bacterial leaf spot, *gray mold*, powdery mildew, southern blight, and verticillium wilt

WALNUTS – Blight, crown gall, oak root fungus, and root rot

Shrubs and Trees

ASHES – Anthracnose and verticillium wilt

AZALEAS AND RHODODENDRONS – Powdery mildew and water mold root rot

CAMELLIAS – *Camellia petal blight*, crown rot, and sooty mold

CLEMATIS – *Fungal stem rot*, fungal wilt, leaf spot, and powdery mildew

CRAPE MYRTLES – Black spot, leaf spot, powdery mildew, root rot, and sooty mold

DOGWOODS – Anthracnose, canker, crown rot, leaf spot, powdery mildew, and twig blight

ELMS – Anthracnose, Dutch elm disease, mosaic viruses, and verticillium wilt

FUCHSIAS – Powdery mildew, rust, and verticillium wilt

HIBISCUS – *Ringspot virus* and root rot

HOLLIES – Anthracnose, canker, crown rot, and root rot

HONEYSUCKLES – Leaf spot, powdery mildew, root rot, and *sooty mold*

HYDRANGEAS – Bacterial wilt, leaf spot, powdery mildew, root rot, and rust

IVIES – Root rot

JUNIPERS – Oak root fungus, *root rot*, rust, and water mold

LILACS – Powdery mildew and verticillium wilt

MAGNOLIAS – Canker, leaf blight, leaf spot mildew, slime flux, and verticillium wilt

MAPLES – Anthracnose, powdery mildew, and verticillium wilt

MULBERRIES – Bacterial canker, leaf spot, powdery mildew, and slime flux

OAKS – Anthracnose, oak root fungus, oak wilt, and powdery mildew

PALMS – Fusarium wilt, heart rot, and *pink rot fungus*

PINES – Fungal rots, needle cast, and rust

ROSES – Black spot, crown gall, downy mildew, gray mold, oak root fungus, powdery mildew, and rust

SPRUCES – Canker, root rot, and rust

SYCAMORES – *Anthracnose*, powdery mildew, and slime flux

WILLOWS – Canker, crown, heart rot, root rot, rust, and twig blight

Vegetables and Herbs

ASPARAGUS – Asparagus rust, gray mold, fusarium wilt, and rust

BEANS – Anthracnose, damping off, downy mildew, fusarium wilt, gray mold, mosaic viruses, powdery mildew, rust, and southern blight

BEETS – *Curly top virus*, downy mildew, fungal leaf spot, root rot, and verticillium wilt

BROCCOLI – Bacterial leaf spot, black rot, *club root*, and downy mildew

CABBAGES – Bacterial soft rot, club root, downy mildew, fusarium wilt, mosaic viruses, powdery mildew, and scab

CANTALOUPES – *See* Melons

CARROTS – Mosaic viruses, powdery mildew, and southern blight

CELERY – Bacterial soft rot, downy mildew, fusarium wilt, and mosaic viruses

CORN – Bacterial wilt, corn smut, leaf and stem blight, and rust

CUCUMBERS – Anthracnose, bacterial wilt, damping off, downy mildew, mosaic viruses, powdery mildew, and verticillium wilt

EGGPLANTS – Anthracnose, bacterial wilt, mosaic viruses, powdery mildew, southern blight, and verticillium wilt

GARLIC – Downy mildew, fusarium rot, pink rot, *smut*, and white rot

LETTUCE – Bacterial leaf spot, gray mold, mosaic viruses, powdery mildew, and southern blight

MELONS – Bacterial leaf spot, bacterial wilt, downy mildew, fusarium wilt, powdery mildew, and verticillium wilt

MINT – Anthracnose, rust, and verticillium wilt

ONIONS – Downy mildew, fusarium wilt, rust, smut, and southern blight

OREGANO – Root rot

PARSLEY – Crown rot and mosaic virus

PEANUTS – Southern blight and verticillium wilt

PEAS – Anthracnose, downy mildew, *fusarium wilt*, mosaic viruses, powdery mildew, and root rot

PEPPERS – Anthracnose, bacterial wilt, fusarium wilt, mosaic viruses, and southern blight

POTATOES – Anthracnose, bacterial wilt, *late blight*, mosaic viruses, scab, southern blight, and verticillium wilt

RADISHES – Black rot, damping off, downy mildew, fusarium wilt, mosaic viruses, scab, and verticillium wilt

SPINACH – Downy mildew, fusarium wilt, mosaic viruses, rust, and verticillium wilt

SQUASHES – Bacterial leaf spot, curly top virus, downy mildew, and powdery mildew

TOMATOES – Anthracnose, bacterial wilt, fusarium wilt, gray mold, mosaic viruses, powdery mildew, southern blight, and verticillium wilt

BACTERIAL CANKER

Have you noticed irregularly shaped, brown water-soaked cankers on your stone fruit trees in early spring? Do these cankers leak a sour-smelling fluid? Sounds like bacterial canker.

A *bacterial disease*

Bacterial canker affects almond, cherry, peach, and other stone fruit trees. The cankers are caused by *Pseudomonas syringae*, bacteria that commonly live on plants. Usually the bacteria don't cause a problem, but when trees are stressed the bacteria can invade open wounds that may have been caused by frost damage, mechanical injury, pruning, leaf scars, and buds. In severe cases the tree will die. Besides cankers, there are other typical signs of the disease: leaves on affected branches will start wilting as the weather becomes warmer or the tree won't leaf out at all.

On apricot and peach trees, the first signs are small purple spots on leaves and black lesions on the fruit. On cherry trees, the first sign is a thick gum oozing from limbs and shoots in spring and fall. The leaves then wilt and die in the summer, and there are dark depressions on the surface of the fruit.

Bacterial canker, besides affecting stone fruit trees, can also affect plants such as tomatoes. The first symptom is wilting of the leaflets and lower leaves. The wilting usually begins on one side of the leaf, then the margins turn dry. Eventually the whole leaf curls upward, turns brown, and dies. Some plants die quickly. On those that survive, cankers form on the stems. Sometimes, small raised snowy dots appear on the surface of the fruit. These dots later break open and appear rough and brown with a white halo around them.

Control

Canker is difficult to control once it has invaded a tree or plant. Basically, there is no cure. Try pruning out infected branches, and be sure to cut a few inches below the site of the canker as well. Always sterilize pruners between cuts. (See page 125 for tool-sterilizing techniques.)

Prevention is really the key. Buy canker-resistant trees if available. Trees planted in shallow soils or soils that are very sandy can become stressed, and stressed trees are more susceptible to canker. When planting, always dig deep holes and amend the soil well. Don't fertilize trees with a nitrogen-rich fertilizer in late summer and fall. Prevent frost damage by covering small trees. Frost can cause wounds that allow the bacteria to enter the tree. And always clean up debris around trees in the fall.

BACTERIAL LEAF SPOT

Some of your garden plants are breaking out in spots. The spots start out tiny but soon grow larger with yellowish halos around them. They then form papery areas. This is bacterial leaf spot.

A bacterial disease

Bacterial leaf spot affects many different types of plants, flowers, and vegetables, including geraniums, poinsettias, celery, cucumbers, and many others. It is caused by *Pseudomonas* and *Xanthomonas* bacteria. The bacteria can live in plant debris from three to six months and spread to plants through tools or splashing water. They thrive in mild, moist conditions in the spring and spread rapidly during periods of fast plant growth. Symptoms vary depending on the plant. The spots may be of different colors. For example, on plants from the cabbage family the spots are black to purplish; tomatoes exhibit minute, water-soaked spots that later become angular and turn black; and on celery the spots look like water-soaked areas that then turn bright yellow.

Control

Avoid overhead watering that can splash the bacteria up and onto plants. Try to avoid handling plants when they are wet to prevent the spread of the disease. Inspect plants often and remove infected leaves or plants when necessary. Destroy infected pruned plant material. If the disease continues to spread, the whole plant or tree may need to be destroyed. Do not plant susceptible plants in the same area again next year. Disinfect all tools regularly.

BLACK SPOT

You know the signs: Ugly black spots on your rose leaves. Sometimes, yellowish edges on the leaves. What can you do to save your beautiful roses?

A rose fungus

Black spot fungus attacks only roses. Those black spots found on the leaves are the fungus itself, not dead spots. It lives on the canes and on fallen dead leaves during the winter and then spreads to the leaves of living roses when the weather is moist or wet. Roses grown in areas in which summers are warm and humid are most likely to suffer black spot.

Control

Start with resistant varieties. Check your nursery for resistant varieties when buying new roses. Raking up dead leaves around the roses you already have planted helps stop the spread of black spot to other roses. When you first notice black spot starting on your plant, apply a baking soda spray to help control the fungus. (See page 24 for easy-to-make solutions.) It is also important to destroy all affected leaves.

Black spot loves moist conditions. Good air circulation around your plants will inhibit black spot on the leaves. Be sure to water your roses early in the day. This gives the plant a chance to dry out during the day. To avoid spreading the fungus yourself, never work on your roses when they are wet. Working around roses only when they are dry lessens the likelihood of spreading. Also, clean all tools with alcohol or bleach after working on affected roses.

DAMPING-OFF DISEASE

Have you noticed that your seeds are not sprouting well and sometimes not sprouting at all? Do the seeds sprout just to die soon after emerging? The culprit could be damping-off disease.

A fungus

The *Sclerotinia* fungus that causes damping off is present in most soils. It may be transported from place to place by garden tools as you bring in topsoil or put soil around potted plants. Its primary targets are seeds and young seedlings; as a plant ages it becomes more resistant. Many different plants can be affected by damping-off disease, including basil, beans, cabbage-family plants, carrots, celery, lettuce, onions, spinach, and tomatoes.

Environmental conditions play a big part in damping-off disease. When the weather is warm and humid and the soil very wet, the conditions are perfect for the fungus. If plants are overcrowded, it can increase the moisture level too, so don't plant too close if you suspect that damping off is a problem.

Unfortunately, there is usually no warning that a plant is infected with damping-off disease. One day the seedlings are fine, and the next day they are all bent over. A soft rot at the soil line weakens the stem. Nothing can be done to stop damping off once it has started. Prevention is the key.

Control

Fresh seeds give the healthiest plants, so start with fresh seeds. Treated seed is now available for better results, but gardeners who are trying to be truly organic may resist buying that kind.

When using recycled pots to start seeds indoors, be sure to wash them well in a bath of 9 parts water and 1 part bleach to kill any fungus.

If you live in cooler climates and start your seeds indoors, use fresh sterile potting soil that drains well. A thin layer of dry material such as sand or fine sphagnum moss on the soil surface will help to keep the seedling's stem dry and reduce the chance of fungal growth. Some gardeners keep a fan blowing gently across the seedlings while indoors to keep air circulating and reduce the humidity around the plants. Transplant the seedlings outside when the weather is warmer and the stems have toughened and can resist the disease. Stems toughen with age, and it depends on the kind of plant as to how long it takes for them to be strong enough to resist disease.

Sometimes it isn't possible to start plants indoors. Plant the seeds when the weather conditions favor growing those particular plants. Resist the temptation to fertilize the young seedlings until they have their first set of true leaves. Damping-off fungi thrive in nitrogen-rich soil. Also, make sure that you are watering properly and that the soil you are planting in drains well. Overwatering can produce the wet conditions that the fungus likes. Like indoors, good air circulation between the plants outdoors also helps keep humid conditions down. Keeping the soil surface acidic also prevents damping off. Dust with fine peat moss or use a mist of chamomile tea to acidify the surface of the soil.

If you still have a problem after trying all of this, then you may have a serious infestation of damping-off fungus in your soil. Soil solarization may be needed. (See page 121 for instructions on solarizing your soil.)

As with any fungal infestation, always follow good sanitation practices. After every use, clean starting pots and flats with bleach or alcohol to prevent the spread of the disease, and always clean your garden tools.

DOWNY MILDEW

There is a kind of fuzzy stuff on the underside of the leaves of many of your vegetables. Some of the leaves have yellow blotches on the tops. Seedlings have purplish lesions on the leaves and stems. Could it be downy mildew? You bet it could!

A fungus

Actually, many fungi cause downy mildew, each attacking a few plant hosts. These fungi are spread by spores via insects, tools, wind, rain, and infected seeds. They flourish in wet conditions. Most also require cool temperatures and high humidity for spore production, although the fungus that infects curcurbits (squash, melons, and cucumbers) can bloom in temperatures up to 90 degrees.

Downy mildew affects many different types of plants, from snapdragons, pansies, roses, and marigolds to strawberries, grapes, and many vegetables. Gray, white, or purplish fuzz grows on the undersides of leaves on infected plants. Sometimes the tops of the leaves look fine. Once plants have contracted the disease they die very quickly.

Control

Keeping the foliage as dry as possible will go a long way in preventing downy mildew. Don't overhead-water or overcrowd the plants. Remove or prune infected plants. Pick off infected leaves and destroy them. Remove plant debris from the garden every fall, and clean tools to prevent the spread of the disease. Do not handle plants when they are wet. Many gardeners recommend a three-year crop rotation as a good preventive measure in areas that are prone to downy mildew. Check with your local nursery for disease-resistant cultivars.

Once the disease is spotted, you can try sulfur, garlic, and baking soda solutions. (See pages 24–25 for spray recipes.)

GRAY MOLD

A tan to gray fuzzy mold is showing up on different plant leaves and stems, and now soft, tan blotches that turn into a rough gray mold are appearing on your tomatoes. It looks like a mold you've seen on old strawberries. Could it be the same one? Yes, indeed!

A fungus

Gray mold is also known as botrytis blight. It attacks many different flowering plants, fruits, and vegetables. The fungus loves shady, crowded conditions. It is very common in cool and humid climates or seasons. The spores of the fungus are spread by the wind and splashing water. The mold usually starts on old fruit or plant tissue and then spreads to healthy tissue. Sometimes the fungus will become slimy looking when the tissue rots.

Control

Don't overcrowd plants in the garden. Allow good air circulation between plants. Water early in the morning to allow the plants to dry out during the day. Pick off dead flowers and leaves to get rid of the primary infection areas. Destroy clippings from infected plants. A dusting of sulfur on infected areas or a foliar spray of compost tea may help to control the mold. (See page 87 for directions on how to make compost tea.)

FIREBLIGHT

Your pear tree looks as if it has been scorched. The leaves and fruit often look wilted and black and are clinging to the tree. On large branches, dark cankers that ooze an orange-brown liquid can be found. Another fungus? No. This time it's a bacterial disease called fireblight.

A bacterial disease

Fireblight affects only members of the rose family. This large plant family includes not only roses but also pears, quince, apple, crabapple, pyracantha, hawthorn, spirea, cotoneaster, toyon, loquat, and mountain ash. The most susceptible members of the family are pears, apples, and quinces.

The bacteria enter through the blossoms and are spread by pollinating insects, aphids and psyllids feeding on new growth, and sometimes water that is splashed around the plants by rainfall or watering. The first symptom of fireblight is that the flowers of the plant or tree start turning brown and then shrivel. The browning begins at the tips of the shoots and progresses toward the roots. The limbs often appear cane-shaped because of the curling at the ends.

Fireblight likes temperatures above 60 degrees and high humidity. It can spread rapidly in warm and humid weather. During winter months it lives in infected bark.

Control

Watch susceptible plants carefully in areas that are prone to fireblight. Avoid overfertilizing, which can cause a flush of new growth that is quite tasty to pest insects that carry the bacteria.

Good sanitation after pruning is important in controlling fireblight because the bacteria can survive in infected twigs and branches. Cut infected branches at least 6 inches below the infection on smaller branches and at least 12 inches below on larger branches. Destroy all infected plant material. Disinfect all pruning tools with bleach or rubbing alcohol.

Clean up any fruit, leaves, or branches that have fallen under trees, especially in the fall. Control aphids and psyllids with a soap or oil spray.

Finally, in areas where fireblight is a problem, look for resistant varieties of plants.

MOSAIC VIRUSES

The leaves of some of your favorite vegetables and flowers look mottled or streaked. The patches are light green, yellow, or white. Flowers have color breaks and some may be disfigured, and some plants even look stunted. What can it be?

A *virus*

There are many different kinds of this common virus. Each one causes a similar type of damage but targets different plants. Some susceptible vegetables are cucumbers, lettuce, melons, peppers, potatoes, raspberries, squash, tomatoes, and watermelons. Many of these viruses are spread by cucumber beetles and sucking insects such as aphids and leafhoppers. The virus overwinters on perennial weeds that are likely to be found around a garden, including chickweed, jimson weed, mints, ragweed, and nightshade.

Some plants with severe cases of mosaic virus have the appearance of the disease but are not affected by it. However, many gardeners like the appearance of the color variations the virus causes. Other plants with the virus do poorly.

Control

Mosaic viruses are incurable, but the spread of the virus can be controlled. First, try to control sucking insects that spread the disease by placing row covers over susceptible plants until they bloom (the disease won't affect flower color after it blooms). Destroy infected plants immediately, and control weeds that might harbor the disease. Do not work around wet plants; you run the risk of spreading the disease. Rotate crops. Finally, buy disease-resistant or certified disease-free plants from the nursery.

OAK ROOT FUNGUS

Does your oak or fruit tree have fan-shaped, tan mushrooms growing around the base in fall or winter? Is there a strong mushroom-smelling fungus under the bark of the tree, close to the soil line? Oak root fungus may be your problem.

A fungus

Oak root fungus is also known as *Armillaria*, shoestring, or mushroom root rot, and it spreads from one tree to another when infected roots come in contact with healthy roots. The fungus can live up to thirty years in roots left underground after an infected tree is cut down. Like others, this fungus likes wet soils and can damage many plants and trees, especially when they are stressed or weakened. The fungus is most common on the West Coast and in the Southeast.

Oak root fungus can live on native oaks without harming them as long as the trees are not watered during the dry season. Infected trees or woody plants usually appear dull, yellowed, or wilted when they are showing early signs of the fungus. The trees may even start to die back slowly.

Control

There is no cure for this disease. When you find signs of this fungus, remove the infected plant or tree and try to remove as many roots as possible. In areas known for oak root fungus, plant resistant varieties.

One treatment that has some effect is to uncover the infected root crown, exposing it to air. Then give the plant little or no water and watch for any signs of improvement.

PEACH TREE CURL

The leaves on your beautiful peach and nectarine trees have blisters and are curling and puckered. Some of them are also tinged with red or yellow. Fruit production is poor. Must be peach tree curl.

A fungus

This fungus (*Taphrina deformans*) is most active during cool and rainy springs. If left untreated, it will weaken the tree, causing branches to die back. Infected leaves may turn yellow and drop early or turn reddish and develop white spores of the fungus that can reinfect the tree the following year. Many times the fruit on heavily infected trees will be deformed or drop early.

Control

Pick off and destroy infected leaves. Apply a spray to kill the fungus before budding, when the trees are dormant in late winter. In fact, to kill all fungal spores it is often recommended that infected trees be sprayed twice, once when the leaves drop and then again before budding in the spring. There are several types of dormant sprays, including lime sulfur and copper fungicides. (See page 54 for a dormant oil spray recipe.)

POWDERY MILDEW

Does it look as if your entire rose plant has been dusted with flour? Have you noticed gray or white circular areas starting to form on your cucumbers? Sounds like powdery mildew is starting to take over.

A fungus

Powdery mildew isn't like most fungi. Most of them like nice, moist soil conditions, but powdery mildew likes dry soil. Warm days with lots of humidity near the plant and cool nights are perfect for this fungus. Wind- or water-borne spores carry powdery mildew to plants.

Not many plants are safe from powdery mildew but among the most susceptible are beans, cucumbers, dahlias, fruit trees, grapes, peas, roses, and some bluegrass lawns. If the disease is left unchecked, the leaves of affected plants may start to drop, weakening the entire plant. The plant then may become stunted and produce low yields. Rarely does powdery mildew kill the whole plant.

Control

Powdery mildew likes dry soil conditions, so up the moisture by watering your plants a little more. Try giving them a spraying of water in the morning to wash off many of the mildew spores. This helps control other fungal infections as well and allows the plants to dry before nightfall.

Prune or pick off affected leaves as soon as you spot the telltale white, powdery areas. Eliminate weedy mildew hosts around your garden. Clean your tools and dispose of affected plant material away from other plants. Spray infected plants with a baking soda mixture as soon as the problem arises. (See page 24 for a good baking soda recipe.)

If you buy your vegetables in pony packs (six seedlings) from your local nursery, look for resistant varieties. New ones are always being developed.

RUST

Do your ornamental plants have yellow or white dots on the upper leaf surface? On the underside of the leaves are there orange to yellow spots or streaks? The problem could be one of the many rust fungi.

Many types of fungi

Rust is a common name for a group of fungi. Rust looks the same on many types of plants, but actually each plant is attacked by a different fungus specific for that plant. So rose rust fungus attacks only roses, and apple rust attacks only apples.

Rust first appears as small pustules on the undersides of leaves. They are generally an orange-yellow color—hence the name of the disease. But some species of rust fungi are not a typical rust color and have purple or brown pustules instead. In any case, your plant looks as if it has a bad case of measles.

Rust can spread fairly quickly, and severely infected plants can become stunted or die. Quick action should be taken when rust is spotted.

Control

Remove all infected parts and dispose of them properly. Keep fallen leaves cleaned up from around healthy plants. If you overhead-water, do it in the morning and give your plants a chance to dry out during the day.

A dusting of sulfur can prevent some rust infestations but sulfur can acidify the soil, so check your soil's pH before applying.

When possible, buy resistant varieties when purchasing new ornamentals. Plant them with plenty of room to allow good air circulation when they mature.

SOOTY MOLD

A thin-looking black substance is coating your favorite orange tree—leaves, fruit, and all. It looks like a mold and wipes off easily. Luckily, the leaf underneath looks healthy. Can it hurt the tree?

A mold indeed

It sounds like sooty mold has indeed taken up residency on your favorite tree. It got its name from its sooty appearance. The mold can live on a plant's natural secretions but the likely cause for the mold's presence is honeydew secreted from sucking insects such as aphids, mealybugs, psyllids, or scales. Any plant with these insects present is at risk of developing sooty mold. Areas that frequently have cool, moist days are at higher risk for sooty mold than other areas.

The mold in sooty mold does not cause a plant disease. However, the black mold that covers the leaves of your plant also prevents the sun's rays from reaching them. This in turn blocks photosynthesis and prevents the plant from making its food, damaging the plant.

Control

The key to controlling sooty mold is controlling the sucking insects. First, give your plant or tree a good hard spraying of water. This will wash away some of the mold and insects. The water will also chase away many of the beneficial insects for a while. Now, while the beneficial insects are gone, add 4 ounces of dishwashing liquid (this amount will treat a large tree) to a hose end sprayer and spray the plant again. This will take off more mold and insects. Always check a plant for burning before using soap spray, but most shiny leaf plants can tolerant soap. It's best to do this early in the morning to give the plant or tree a chance to dry out during the day and thus avoid causing other problems.

For small sooty mold infestations, simply wiping the leaves will get rid of the mold and the insects.

SOUTHERN BLIGHT

Suddenly you notice a white, cottony-looking growth on the stems of your plants. Most of it is located near the soil level and even appears to be in the soil itself. It looks pretty strange. What can it be?

A fungus

Anyone living in the southeastern region of the United States has probably come into contact with southern blight at one time or another. This fungus lives in the soil and basically rots a plant's stems. It loves the warm and wet conditions of the southern climate and can be rather difficult to control.

Southern blight is probably the most common name, but this fungus is also known as southern wilt, *Sclerotium* root rot, and mustard-seed fungus. It attacks many flowering plants, grasses, and vegetables. Peanuts and tomatoes and their relatives are particular favorites of the fungus.

The fungus hurts the plant as it grows, constricting the flow of water. As the stems become progressively clogged, the plant can't get enough water and wilts and dies. A good way to identify this fungus is to look for the organisms' small, yellowish resting bodies, which will be present on the plant and look like mustard seeds.

Control

This is not an easy fungus to control, especially if you must put your tomato plant in that nice sunny spot that was infected last year. Generally a two- to three-year crop rotation plan is the first step in getting rid of this fungus. Alternate every other year with immune plants—corn, for example—to break the cycle. Then increase the nitrogen content of the soil with a good organic fertilizer or manure to suppress the fungus.

Plants can get some protection if you wrap aluminum foil along their stems before planting. The foil should extend from just above the roots to about two inches above the soil line for seedlings. For larger transplants the foil should extend from two to three inches below the soil line to two to three inches above. This works pretty well as a physical barrier against the fungus on tomatoes and peppers.

Aluminum foil or other light-reflective material can also be used to scare away aphids and thrips, which carry this fungus and other viruses. To do this, spread a thirty-inch-wide piece of the material on the soil surrounding susceptible plants like squash.

When you spot an infected plant, remove the entire plant and at least eight inches of soil from all around it. Place discarded plant material in plastic bags and allow the sun to bake and kill the fungus before discarding the material.

VERTICILLIUM WILT

Have you noticed that one side of your plant has started to turn yellow while the other side looks fine? Generally the leaf edges start yellowing and turning brown at the base of the plant and then the problem continues upward and outward, finally causing the whole plant to wilt. Or perhaps your plant looked healthy until the weather turned warm and dry, and then it went downhill fast.

Another fungus?

Yes, it sounds like the dreaded verticillium wilt. This disease will attack more than two hundred plant species, including tomatoes, potatoes, and strawberries. It is a fungus that lives in the soil and causes damage by plugging water-conducting vessels in the plant.

It loves cool, moist soils, but usually the damage isn't noticed until the weather turns warm and drier. A quick check of the tissue inside a dead plant stem or branch will confirm the fungus. The tissue will be very discolored if it is verticillium.

Verticillium overwinters in plant debris, fallen fruit, and the soil, making it difficult to control just by keeping the garden clean of debris. It can be transmitted to plants by watering or during cultivation. In addition, several weed species—like chickweed, horse nettle, jimson weed, mints, and ragweed—can harbor verticillium and spread the fungus to susceptible plants.

Control

Verticillium can live for twenty years in the soil. To combat this hard-to-control disease, resistant plant varieties have been developed and many nurseries sell them. Check with your local nursery to find out which plants are resistant. A "V" symbol is usually marked on the plant's label to indicate this. If the plant you want doesn't come in a resistant variety and you know your soil has verticillium, then you will need to plan ahead.

Verticillium usually only lives in the top six inches of soil. So, first consider getting rid of the top six inches of your soil and replacing it with fresh, clean topsoil. If this isn't an option for you, then consider soil solarization. Do not till the soil before putting the plastic down: solarization is usually only effective in the first six inches of soil, where the verticillium likes to live, and tilling might mix the fungus down deeper.

If your soil has only a light infestation of verticillium, reducing nitrogen fertilizers and maintaining a soil high in organic matter can help. Good garden sanitation will also go a long way in preventing the spread of verticillium. Clean all garden tools with alcohol or bleach to kill any fungus on the tools and prevent its spread.

Although some gardening books advocate for it, using crop rotation to control the disease doesn't work. Because the disease is so long-lived, unless you don't plant anything for twenty years, it will still be there in the soil, waiting for you to plant one of its favorite varieties.

Finally, try planting marigolds! This lovely garden flower has many virtues. Already well known for its pest-repelling properties, an entomologist at Montana State University has found that it also helps control the fungus that causes verticillium wilt. Florence Dunkel showed that when marigolds were planted and then plowed under in a field inoculated with verticillium wilt, this protected mint plants, which are susceptible to verticillium wilt, the next year. If you live in an area where verticillium wilt is a problem, Dunkel suggests planting a variety such as African marigold (*Tagetes erecta*) in April. Then, in June, turn the marigolds under with a shovel or tiller. Now plant your crop. Repeat as necessary.

WATER MOLD ROOT ROT

Your lovely bushes were looking just fine. Now the leaves look dull and some are even yellowing and wilting. The bush just seems to be losing its vigor, even though you are careful to water it a lot.

A fungus

Most fungi love wet conditions, and overwatering can produce just such conditions. If the soil your bush is planted in doesn't drain well and water stands too long at the base and around its roots, then your bush is at risk of developing water mold root rot, a condition that is caused by a variety of fungi.

The fungi start a rot that invades the roots and then works its way up the plant. This can be a quick or slow process, depending on conditions. Often after the rot is established you will see dark discolorations in the plant's roots and stems. This is where the infected plant tissue meets healthy tissue. Sometimes the plant will also appear girdled at or below ground level.

Control

Again, there is no cure for this disease, so once your bush is infected there is little you can do but remove it. But before you plant another bush in its place, apply a bit of prevention.

Make sure the area drains properly. Good drainage will prevent the wet conditions the fungi love. Add soil amendments as needed by your type of soil. For heavily infected soils, try soil solarization.

Plant the new bush at the right depth and water it only enough to promote healthy growth; do not overwater.

FUNGUS-KILLING SPRAYS

Many fungal diseases can be controlled with fungal sprays that can be made from simple ingredients you are likely to have around the house. Here are a few good recipes.

BAKING SODA

The same baking soda that you use for cooking makes a great spray to combat fungi that attack plants. Brown rot on grapes and mildew on roses are just a few of the fungal problems that baking soda sprays will help cure; a variation of the basic recipe works best for rust.

Basic soda spray

2 tablespoons baking soda

1 gallon water

Optional: 1 teaspoon sticker/spreader (available at garden shops), or liquid car wax, or vegetable oil

Mix ingredients together and spray solution on problem areas. Repeat as necessary.

Soda spray for rust

2 tablespoons baking soda

1 gallon water

6 tablespoons horticultural or vegetable oil

2 tablespoons kelp extract

Mix ingredients together and spray solution on rust-covered areas. Repeat as necessary.

GARLIC

Garlic is known to fight many types of disease-causing fungi, including downy mildew, powdery mildew, gray mold, and rust. Garlic has not only been shown to fight fungi but also has some repellent qualities for other diseases and even insects.

Basic garlic spray

1 garlic bulb

1 quart water

Crush bulb of garlic and place it in pan with water. Bring to a boil, then turn off the heat. Let mixture cool. Strain out garlic. Pour liquid into a spray bottle, and spray affected areas of the plant. Repeat as necessary.

VINEGAR

Use apple cider vinegar to make a great spray to combat many fungal diseases, including black spot on roses.

Vinegar spray

3 tablespoons apple cider vinegar
1 gallon water

Mix vinegar and water together. Spray mixture on plants, being sure to do so in the morning so the plant has time to dry out before evening. Repeat as necessary.

LAWN DISEASES, SYMPTOMS, AND CONTROLS

Some of the most frequently asked questions of plant professionals have to do with lawns. We Americans love our lawns and want them to look like gorgeous golf courses or the lawns in those "do-everything" fertilizer commercials. Many people think that if they decide to go organic, they will never have a beautiful lawn again. Wrong! Armed with some organic basics, your lawn can be as lush and beautiful as the house next door's.

START WITH THE SOIL

Good gardeners know that great vegetables come from good, rich soil. So does great grass. If you have an existing lawn that doesn't look very good, chances are the soil has a problem. Many people never think of having their soil tested for lawns, but it is a good idea.

A soil test will tell you several things. The most important finding is the organic matter content of the soil. This is important, because it is the organic matter that holds water and nutrients, lets oxygen reach the roots, and feeds the microorganisms that make essential nutrients available for healthy grass. If your test shows less than 5 percent organic matter, add a ¼-inch layer of compost over the lawn every fall to increase it. Use a mulching lawnmower, or just leave the clippings where they fall to decompose and add more organic matter. Don't rake the leaves before mowing, either. The mower will cut them into tiny pieces that will break down quickly.

A soil test will also show the levels of nutrients in the soil. Grass likes a K-Mg-Ca level of 1-3-21 (that is, by weight, 1 percent potassium, 3 percent magnesium, and 21 percent calcium). A good organic fertilizer can help here if needed.

The soil test will also show the soil's pH level—how acidic or alkaline it is. The scale runs from 1 to 14, with 7 being neutral. A low number means the soil is very acidic, a high number very alkaline. The pH of the soil affects the capacity of roots to take up nutrients. Lawns thrive in a pH of 6.8. Lawn professionals recommend adding lime if the pH is low, and sulfur if the pH is high. Always check the recommended doses on each package, and follow directions carefully to avoid burning your lawn.

The soil test will not measure for nitrogen, but this is still an important nutrient for lawns. We usually overfertilize our lawns with nitrogen. The recommended dose is this: no more than four pounds (per 1,000 square feet) of nitrogen should be added to a lawn in one year and no more than one pound should be added at any one time.

Here is a simple calculation to use when applying nitrogen fertilizer: A twenty-pound bag of fertilizer with 5 percent nitrogen will deliver one pound of actual nitrogen to the lawn. If you have added compost and clippings to the lawn over the year, then you will need less nitrogen fertilizer. Compost and clippings supply about two pounds of nitrogen a year.

KNOW WHAT KIND OF GRASS YOU HAVE

Is your grass a fescue or bluegrass? Maybe it's a blend? This may sound like an obvious question, but many people don't know the answer. You may be surprised to know that 1,500 different grass species grow in the United States and about forty of them are cultivated for lawns. If you don't know what yours is, take a sample of your lawn to a garden professional or county agriculture extension office. When you have a new seed lawn put in, ask for the label from the package of seed. Or ask your gardener, landscaper, or sod dealer what kinds of grass or grasses are in your new sod lawn.

IS YOUR LAWN STRESSED OUT?

Sometimes lawn problems have nothing to do with the grass itself, but other factors cause the grass to be unhealthy for one reason or another. Stress is the biggest cause of lawn problems. A stressed lawn can't resist diseases and insects as well a healthy lawn can.

Here's a checklist to help you figure out what might be causing your lawn to be stressed.

Does your grass grow well in your climate type?

The United States is generally divided into two grass-growing climates, and certain grasses do better in each one. A kind of wavy line basically divides the country down the middle into north and south. Cool-season grasses grow better in the northern states, and subtropical grasses grow better in the southern states. If you live somewhere in the middle, check with a lawn professional, garden center, or county agriculture extension office to determine which type of grass would be best suited for your climate. Actually, our favorite method for determining the best type of grass is to drive around a neighborhood and look for a well-established, good-looking lawn, and then ask what it is. The owners are usually happy to brag about a good-looking lawn.

Cool-season grasses include bluegrass, fescue, bent, and rye grasses, to name a few. Although these grasses generally do well in the cooler northern climates, they can also be found in lawns in the South. They are usually planted from seed and are often blended together.

Subtropical grasses include Bermuda, centipede, zoysia, St. Augustine, and Bahia. These grasses are usually grown from stolons (stems that run along the ground and can form roots), sprigs, plugs, or sod. They love the warm summer weather, but they go dormant if the weather turns too cool.

Are you watering your lawn properly?

A lawn that is lacking water will often look dull or smoky green in color. However, a lawn that is overwatered is under great stress. Soggy soils deprive the grass roots of needed oxygen and encourages many fungal diseases, which love wet or damp conditions. Many factors come into play here, such as soil type, what kind of grass you have, your climate, the season, and how you apply the water. Most professionals agree that watering a lawn thoroughly and infrequently is best. By doing this you promote deep grass root growth. Light sprinklings daily promote shallow root growth, and in the end, more and more water is required to feed the surface roots. Deep roots need less water because the soil loses moisture less rapidly. The easiest way to test moisture in the soil is to plunge a long trowel or shovel into the lawn to see how far down the wetness goes. If the shovel goes down easily, the soil is adequately moist.

Soil type too affects watering. Sandy soils allow water to move faster and deeper than clay soils; loam soils are somewhere in between. Clay soils hold water better than sandy soils. The general rule for grasses grown in heavier clay soils is deep, once-a-week watering, because the clay will hold the water. Grass grown in lighter soils benefit from more frequent, low-volume watering. Check lawn and soil for good root growth and adjust watering accordingly. Some sandy soils hold very little water. If you don't know what kind of soil you have, you can have it tested for a small fee, or simply do the pinch test: Just rub a pinch of moist soil between your thumb and forefinger. If the soil is sandy, it will feel gritty. Silty soil feels smooth and slick, and clay soil feels sticky and rolls up easily. The ideal soil, loam, will feel mealy, because it is about 50 percent sand and between 25 and 50 percent each silt and clay.

Are you watering enough, but the water is standing on the surface or running off?

In this case, soil compaction—caused by a lot of foot traffic or a buildup of thatch beneath the grass—may be the problem. Opening the soil and adding more organic matter may be all that is needed. Organic matter will encourage earthworms, which benefit the lawn by eating and breaking down the thatch.

Do you have a tree in your lawn?

Your tree may be casting too much shade. Thin the tree out a bit. Trees can also be moisture and nutrient robbers. Be sure to water poor-looking grass under a tree more than elsewhere and fertilize the area with a good organic fertilizer at least three times a year. When you mow the lawn, let the grass under a tree remain a bit longer than elsewhere.

Does the lawn have small dead spots?

Small dead spots surrounded by a ring of very green grass may be a sign that a female dog is visiting your lawn. Give these areas extra water and sprinkle on a handful of agricultural gypsum, and it is likely that the lawn will come back as good as new. Gypsum allows water to penetrate the soil and helps leach out the salts from the urine.

Have your neighbors been spraying chemicals on their lawn?

Check to see if chemicals sprayed next door have blown onto your lawn. Damage from spray drift often looks streaky or fan-shaped. Generally a lawn will recover from the damage.

Does one area look bad while the rest of the lawn looks fine?

Perhaps you have tried everything in the past year, but that spot still just doesn't look good. Check to see if there are any low or high spots across your lawn. Either of these conditions can cause the grass there to appear different from the rest of your lawn. High spots may get too little water, low spots too much. Even out such areas.

How are you cutting your lawn?

Don't cut your lawn too short, and keep your lawnmower blade sharp. Many grasses are healthiest at about 3½ to 4 inches tall, but a few will topple over at that height. Mow fescues and centipede grasses ½ inch shorter. If your lawn is overgrown because it hasn't been mowed in a while—perhaps you were away on vacation—remember never to take off more than ⅓ of the grass blades at any one mowing.

If you have tried all these tips to relieve stress on your lawn and still have a problem, it is time to look for a lawn disease as the possible cause. The following table lists the most common forms of fungal lawn diseases and ways to help control them.

Common Fungal Lawn Diseases and Controls

Disease	Symptoms	Susceptible Grasses	Controls
Brown patch	Small, irregularly shaped brown spots that may enlarge as disease strengthens. Centers of spots may recover, exposing large brown circles (like smoke rings) in the lawn. Blades become water soaked, turn yellowish brown, and die.	Bent grasses, Bermudas, bluegrasses, fescues, ryegrasses, zoysia	Minimize shade. Aerate lawn. Irrigate 6 inches deep, as needed. Avoid fertililizers high in nitrogen.
Dollar spot	Many small (2-inch or so) brown spots first appear in the lawn. Blades have tan blotches with reddish brown margins. Sometimes spots merge to make large, straw-colored areas. Dieback from tip. Dew-covered grass often reveals a cobwebby growth on the spots. Mainly occurs during warm wet weather.	Bent grasses, Bermudas, bluegrasses, fescues, ryegrasses	Rake lawns to improve aeration. Keep deep watering to a minimum. Apply a fertilizer high in nitrogen if there is a nitrogen deficiency. Don't walk on grass and disinfect all tools. Water only in the mornings to let lawn dry completely.

Disease	Symptoms	Susceptible Grasses	Controls
Fairy ring	Small circular patches of dark green grass, often with dead grass inside rings. Mushrooms that come up along the margins may or may not be present, but if present are a clear sign of this disease. Major problem in acid soils. Fungi are growing on organic matter in the soil and can cause grass next to mushrooms to dry out and die.	All grasses	Aerate lawns. Apply a fertilizer high in nitrogen. Water and mow more often. Soak rings with water for several weeks to a month. No chemical control.
Fusarium patch	Brown spots 2 to 12 inches in diameter. Look for weblike threads in grass thatch or on dead blades. Same webby fungal threads can be seen on dew-covered grass.	Bluegrasses, creeping bent grasses, fescues, ryegrasses, zoysia	Minimize shade. Aerate lawn. Improve drainage. Avoid fertilizers high in nitrogen.
Grease spot, pythium, or cottony blight	Infected grass blades turn dark and become matted together, giving the appearance of greasy streaks through the lawn. Sometimes a white cottony mold appears on leaf blades. Blades can also have white fungal threads. Spots can spread quickly and the grass will turn a reddish brown, then tan. Worse in hot and humid weather. Spreads quickly through watering, mowing, and foot traffic.	All grasses, especially top-seeded grasses, bluegrasses, and ryegrasses	Minimize shade. Aerate lawn. Do not overwater. Improve drainage and sanitize tools. Most controls have little effect; prevention is the key.
Leaf spot	Infected area shows patches of brown, thin grass. Small oval spots with bright red centers and darker borders will show on grass blades. Lawns under stress are most susceptible.	Bluegrasses, ryegrasses	Rake lawns to remove thatch. Reduce water if lawn is very wet. Don't mow too low.

Disease	Symptoms	Susceptible Grasses	Controls
Melting out	A gradual, indefinite yellowing in the lawn. In infected areas, look for bright yellow grass blades with brown spots and darkened borders. Eventually the whole blade turns brown.	Kentucky bluegrass	Minimize shade. Aorate lawn. Improve drainage. Mow no shorter than 1¾ inches.
Red thread	Strands of pink fungus threads bind blades together. Lawn yellows in patches 2 to 12 inches in diameter. Occurs from late fall through winter into early spring in wet climates. Short pink forked threads coming from the tips of the diseased grass blades are a sure indication of this fungus.	Bent grasses, bluegrasses, fescues, ryegrasses	Do not apply a fertilizer high in nitrogen in late fall. Instead, fertilize lawn regularly with a fertilizer containing nitrogen, potassium and phosphate. Water deeply and infrequently. Minimize shade and increase air circulation.
Rust	Small reddish pustules form on older leaf blades and stems. Blades shrivel and die. Rub a white cloth over a suspected infection; if the cloth picks up an orange color, it is rust. Rust is most active in moist conditions.	Bluegrasses, ryegrasses	Apply a fertilizer high in nitrogen. Water regularly in the morning. Minimize shade.

Disease	Symptoms	Susceptible Grasses	Controls
Slime mold	Grass is covered with tiny, powdery balls that may be bluish gray, whitish, or yellow. The fungi feed on decaying matter in the soil. Damage, if any, is caused by the fungi blocking light to the grass, which can turn the grass yellowish. Mostly occurs in humid or rainy conditions on the East and West Coasts.	All grasses	To get rid of the slime, just hose or sweep the grass.
Snow mold	White-gray, tan, yellowing, or pink patches appear in the lawn. There are several varieties. Margins between these patches are distinct. Dead grass pulls up easily. Most common in early spring when snow melts. Grass blades look stuck together.	Bluegrasses, bent grasses, fescues, and most other grasses	Avoid applying fertilizers in the late fall. Keep lawn aerated to avoid drainage problems. Improve drainage. Mow frequently. Reduce snow pile-up and remove snow from lawn as soon as possible. Rake after removing snow.
Tip burn or septoria leaf spot	The grass blade tips turn a pale yellow to gray and have tiny black dots with red or yellow margins. Appears mostly in cool, wet conditions in spring and fall.	Bermuda, cool-season grasses	Mow to remove tips.

Pest Control Solutions for the Garden and Lawn

Nothing is quite as depressing to a gardener than walking out in the morning to see that your flowers or vegetables have been chewed by insects. This chapter will discuss when to take action, and how to use beneficial insects to fight the insect pests in your garden. If a more direct approach is needed, instructions on how to make traps and control sprays are included to help you win the war over the pests.

The following is an alphabetical list of common plants and the pests that love them. If known, the most common pest is italicized.

COMMON PLANT, VEGETABLE, AND TREE PESTS

Flowers

ASTERS – Aphids, *blister beetles*, cucumber beetles, European corn borers, leafhoppers, slugs, snails, tarnished plant bugs, thrips, and whiteflies

BEGONIAS – Aphids, *mealybugs*, nematodes, slugs, snails, spider mites, thrips, and whiteflies

CALENDULAS – Aphids, cabbage loopers, corn earworms, cutworms, leafhoppers, and spider mites

CARNATIONS – Aphids, cabbage loopers, cutworms, mealybugs, slugs, snails, spider mites, spittlebugs, and thrips

CHRYSANTHEMUMS – Aphids, cabbage loopers, corn earworms, *cucumber beetles*, cutworms, European corn borers, lacebugs, leaf miners, nematodes, slugs, snails, spider mites, tarnished plant bugs, thrips, and whiteflies

COSMOS – Aphids, beetles, borers, leafhoppers, spider mites, and thrips

DAHLIAS – Aphids, cucumber beetles, European corn borers, leafhoppers, leaf miners, nematodes, slugs, snails, and tarnished plant bugs

DELPHINIUMS – Aphids, *cutworms*, leafhoppers, slugs, snails, spider mites, and thrips

GERANIUMS – Aphids, *geranium budworms*, mealybugs, slugs, snails, spider mites, and whiteflies

GLADIOLUS – Aphids, cutworms, European corn borers, spider mites, tarnished plant bugs, and *thrips*

HOLLYHOCKS – Aphids, European corn borers, leafhoppers, mealybugs, nematodes, slugs, snails, spider mites, thrips, and whiteflies

IMPATIENS – Aphids, cucumber beetles, mealybugs, nematodes, scale insects, slugs, snails, spider mites, and tarnished plant bugs

IRIS – Aphids, borers, nematodes, slugs, snails, spider mites, thrips, weevils, whiteflies, and wireworms

LILIES – Aphids, mealybugs, *nematodes*, root maggots, scale insects, slugs, snails, spider mites, and thrips

MARIGOLDS – Cabbage loopers, cutworms, leaf miners, slugs, snails, spider mites, and *tarnished plant bugs*

NARCISSUS – Aphids, mealybugs, mites, *narcissus bulb flies*, nematodes, slugs, snails, and thrips

PANSIES – Aphids, cutworms, flea beetles, mealybugs, nematodes, slugs, snails, spider mites, and *wireworms*

PEONIES – *Rose chafers* and thrips

PETUNIAS – Armyworms, blister beetles, *cabbage loopers*, Colorado potato beetles, flea beetles, geranium budworms, hornworms, slugs, and snails

PHLOX – Aphids, leafhoppers, spider mites, and wireworms

POPPIES – Aphids, *corn earworms*, leafhoppers, mealybugs, rose chafers, slugs, snails, and tarnished plant bugs

PRIMROSES – Leaf miners, slugs, snails, spider mites, and whiteflies

SNAPDRAGONS – Aphids, cabbage loopers, corn earworms, nematodes, slugs, snails, and spider mites

SWEET PEAS – Aphids, slugs, and snails

TULIPS – Aphids, spider mites, and wireworms

ZINNIAS – Aphids, blister beetles, cucumber beetles, European corn borers, flea beetles, Japanese beetles, mealybugs, and tarnished plant bugs

Fruit Trees, Bushes, and Vines

APPLES – Aphids, borers, cankerworms, cicadas, *codling moths*, cucumber beetles, fall webworms, fruit flies, green fig beetles, gypsy moths, Japanese beetles, leafhoppers, leaf miners, leaf rollers, mealybugs, psyllids, sawflies, scale insects, spider mites, tarnished plant bugs, tent caterpillars, thrips, tussock moths, and weevils

APRICOTS – Aphids, borers, codling moths, green fig beetles, plum curculios, scale insects, spider mites, and whiteflies

BLACKBERRIES AND RASPBERRIES – Aphids, borers, cutworms, fruit flies, Japanese beetles, leafhoppers, leaf rollers, psyllids, *red-berry mites*, root weevils, sawflies, scale insects, thrips, and whiteflies

BLUEBERRIES – Fruit flies, Japanese beetles, nematodes, scale insects, and weevils

CHERRIES – Aphids, borers, cankerworms, fall webworms, fruit flies, gypsy moths, Japanese beetles, leaf rollers, nematodes, plum curculios, sawflies, scale insects, spider mites, tent caterpillars, and tussock moths

CITRUS – Ants, aphids, leaf rollers, mealybugs, mites, scale insects, and whiteflies

CURRANTS – Aphids, borers, and fruit flies

FIGS – Ants and green fig beetles

GRAPES – Aphids, armyworms, borers, *grape leaf skeletonizers*, Japanese beetles, leafhoppers, leaf rollers, mealybugs, nematodes, rose chafers, scale insects, spider mites, thrips, and whiteflies

PEACHES AND NECTARINES – Aphids, borers, cankerworms, cicadas, curculios, fall webworms, fruit flies, green fig beetles, Japanese beetles, leaf rollers, mealybugs, nematodes, scale insects, spider mites, tarnished plant bugs, tent caterpillars, thrips, and tussock moths

PEARS – Aphids, borers, cankerworms, codling moths, curculios, flea beetles, fruit flies, leaf miners, leaf rollers, mealybugs, *psyllids*, sawflies, scale insects, spider mites, tarnished plant bugs, tent caterpillars, thrips, and tussock moths

PLUMS AND PRUNES – Aphids, borers, cankerworms, curculios, fruit flies, Japanese beetles, leaf rollers, mealybugs, sawflies, scale insects, spider mites, tent caterpillars, and tussock moths

QUINCES – Aphids, *borers*, codling moths, fall webworms, scale insects, and tent caterpillars

STRAWBERRIES – Aphids, cutworms, flea beetles, leaf rollers, mealybugs, nematodes, root weevils, scale insect, slugs, snails, spider mites, sowbugs, tarnished plant bugs, thrips, and wireworms

WALNUTS – Aphids, caterpillars, codling moths, leaf rollers, scales, spider mites, and *walnut husk flies*

Shrubs and Trees

ASHES – Aphids, borers, lacebugs, scale insects, tent caterpillars, and whiteflies

AZALEAS AND RHODODENDRONS – Aphids, borers, lacebugs, leafminers, root weevils, scale insects, spider mites, thrips, and whiteflies

CAMELLIAS – Aphids, leaf galls, and scale insects

CLEMATIS – Earwigs, slugs, and snails

CRAPE MYRTLES – Aphids and scale insects

DOGWOODS – Borers, cicadas, leafhoppers, and scale insects

ELMS – Aphids, bark beetles, borers, cankerworms, elm leaf beetles, leafhoppers, leaf rollers, and scale insects

FUCHSIAS – Aphids, *fuchsia mites*, mealybugs, and whiteflies

HIBISCUS – Aphids, beetles, mealybugs, scale insects, and *whiteflies*

HOLLIES – Beetles, moths, leaf miners, nematodes, scale insects, spider mites, and whiteflies

HONEYSUCKLES – Aphids, flea beetles, mealybugs, mites, scale insects, and whiteflies

HYDRANGEAS – Aphids, scale insects, slugs, and snails

IVIES – Aphids, scale insects, slugs, and snails

JUNIPERS – Aphids, bagworms, borers, leaf miners, scale insects, and spider mites

LILACS – Aphids, borers, cucumber beetles, leaf miners, mealybugs, scale insects, spider mites, and whiteflies

MAGNOLIAS – Loopers, mealybugs, scale insects, and thrips

MAPLES – Aphids, bagworms, borers, cankerworms, gypsy moths, leafhoppers, mealybugs, nematodes, scale insects, spider mites, thrips, and whiteflies

MULBERRIES – *Fall webworms*, mites, nematodes, scale insects, and whiteflies

OAKS – Aphids, bark beetles, borers, cankerworms, cicadas, gall wasps, gypsy moths, Japanese beetles, lacebugs, leaf miners, leaf rollers, scale insects, spider mites, tent caterpillars, tussock moths, and whiteflies

PALMS – Borers, leaf skeletonizers, mealybugs, nematodes, scale insects, spider mites, and thrips

PINES – Aphids, bark beetles, borers, nematodes, sawflies, scale insects, and spider mites

ROSES – Aphids, borers, corn earworms, cucumber beetles, curculios, fall webworms, harlequin bugs, Japanese beetles, leafhoppers, leaf rollers, nematodes, rose chafers, sawflies, scale insects, slugs, snails, spider mites, thrips, and whiteflies

SPRUCES – Aphids, borers, budworms, needle miners, sawflies, scale insects, spider mites, and weevils

SYCAMORES – Aphids, borers, lacebugs, psyllids, and scale insects

WILLOWS – Aphids, borers, fall webworms, sawflies, scale insects, and tussock moths

Vegetables and Herbs

ASPARAGUS – Aphids, *asparagus beetles*, harlequin bugs, Japanese beetles, slugs, snails, spider mites, and tarnished plant bugs

BASIL – Cutworms

BEANS – Aphids, armyworms, blister beetles, corn earworms, cucumber beetles, cutworms, European corn borers, flea beetles, harlequin bugs, Japanese beetles, leafhoppers, leaf miners, mealybugs, Mexican bean beetles, nematodes, slugs, snails, spider mites, tarnished plant bugs, thrips, weevils, whiteflies, and wireworms

BEETS – Aphids, armyworms, blister beetles, flea beetles, leafhoppers, leaf miners, nematodes, webworms, and wireworms

BROCCOLI – Aphids, cabbageworms, cabbage loopers, cabbage root maggots, cutworms, and flea beetles

CABBAGES AND OTHER CABBAGE-FAMILY CROPS, SUCH AS KOHLRABI, BRUSSELS SPROUTS, AND CAULIFLOWER – Aphids, armyworms, blister beetles, cabbage loopers, cutworms, earwigs, flea beetles, *harlequin bugs*, imported cabbageworms, leaf miners, nematodes, root maggots, root weevils, slugs, snails, symphylans, tarnished plant bugs, and thrips

CANTALOUPES – *See* Cucumbers

CARROTS – Aphids, blister beetles, *carrot rust flies*, flea beetles, leafhoppers, parsley worms, root-knot nematodes, root weevils, thrips, and wireworms

CELERY – Aphids, cabbage loopers, flea beetles, leafhoppers, mites, nematodes, parsleyworms, root weevils, slugs, tarnished plant bugs, and thrips

CHIVES – *See* Onions

CORN – Aphids, armyworms, blister beetles, chinch bugs, *corn earworms*, cucumber beetle larvae, cutworms, earwigs, European corn borers, flea beetles, harlequin bugs, Japanese beetles, June beetles, nematodes, and wireworms

CUCUMBERS AND OTHER MEMBERS OF THE CUCURBITS FAMILY, SUCH AS MELON, PUMPKIN, AND SQUASH – Aphids, blister beetles, *cucumber beetles*, flea beetles, harlequin bugs, leafhoppers, nematodes, spider mites, squash bugs, squash vine borers, tarnished plant bugs, thrips, and whiteflies

DILL – Aphids and *parsleyworms*

EGGPLANTS – Aphids, blister beetles, Colorado potato beetles, cutworms, flea beetles, harlequin bugs, hornworms, leafhoppers, nematodes, potato tuberworms, spider mites, and whiteflies

FENNEL – Parsleyworms and slugs

GARLIC – Aphids, nematodes, onion maggots, root maggots, and thrips

LETTUCE – Aphids, armyworms, cabbage loopers, corn earworms, flea beetles, harlequin bugs, leafhoppers, leaf miners, slugs, snails, tarnished plant bugs, and whiteflies

MELONS – *See* Cucumbers

MINT – Aphids, borers, cutworms, flea beetles, loopers, nematodes, spider mites, and weevils

OKRA – Fire ants, green fig beetles, Japanese beetles, and nematodes

ONIONS AND OTHER ONION FAMILY CROPS, SUCH AS LEEKS AND CHIVES – Blister beetles, cutworms, green fig beetles, nematodes, onion maggots, thrips, and wireworms

OREGANO – *Aphids*, leaf miners, and spider mites

PARSLEY – Parsleyworms

PEAS – Aphids, armyworms, blister beetles, cabbage loopers, corn earworms, cucumber beetles, flea beetles, leafhoppers, nematodes, spider mites, thrips, and weevils

PEPPERS – Aphids, blister beetles, Colorado potato beetles, corn earworms, European corn borers, flea beetles, hornworms, leafhoppers, leaf miners, leaf rollers, nematodes, potato tuberworms, spider mites, and whiteflies

POTATOES – Aphids, blister beetles, cabbage loopers, Colorado potato beetles, cucumber beetles, European corn borers, flea beetles, harlequin bugs, hornworms, June beetles, leafhoppers, leaf miners, nematodes, potato tuberworms, psyllids, root maggots, root weevils, tarnished plant bugs, and wireworms

PUMPKINS – *See* Cucumbers

RADISHES – *Cabbage root maggots*, flea beetles, and harlequin bugs

RHUBARB – Caterpillars, Japanese beetles, leafhoppers, and slugs

SPINACH – Aphids, blister beetles, cabbage loopers, flea beetles, imported cabbageworms, leafhoppers, leaf miners, and root weevils

SQUASH – Aphids, cucumber beetles, leafhoppers, nematodes, squash vine borers, and spider mites

SWEET POTATOES – Aphids, flea beetles, nematodes, sweet potato weevils, and wireworms

SWISS CHARD – Aphids, armyworms, blister beetles, flea beetles, grasshoppers, leafhoppers, and leaf miners

TOMATOES – Aphids, armyworms, blister beetles, cabbage loopers, Colorado potato beetles, corn earworms, cucumber beetles, cutworms, European corn borers, flea beetles, hornworms, leafhoppers, nematodes, potato tuberworms, psyllids, slugs, snails, spider mites, thrips, and whiteflies

TURNIPS – Aphids, cabbage root maggots, flea beetles, and *wireworms*

COMMON LAWN GRASS PESTS

BENT GRASS – Chinch bugs, cutworms, grubs, mole crickets, and sod webworms

BERMUDA GRASS – Armyworms, sowbugs, cutworms, grubs, mealybugs, *mites*, nematodes, and sod webworms

BUFFALO GRASS – Chinch bugs, mealybugs, mites, and webworms

DICHONDRA – Cutworms, *flea beetles*, nematodes, slugs, snails, and spider mites

FESCUE – Chinch bugs, cutworms, *grubs*, leafhoppers, and sod webworms

KENTUCKY BLUEGRASS – Chinch bugs, cutworms, grubs, leafhoppers, and sod webworms

RYEGRASS (ANNUAL) – Cutworms, grubs, and leafhoppers

RYEGRASS (PERENNIAL) – Cutworms, grubs, leafhoppers, and sod webworms

ST. AUGUSTINE GRASS – Armyworms, chinch bugs, cutworms, grubs, mole crickets, and sod webworms

ZOYSIA – Armyworms, billbugs, *chinch bugs*, grubs, and sod webworms

CONTROL THE PEST OR LET NATURE TAKE ITS COURSE?

For many gardeners, a good offense is better than a good defense. As soon as the first seed is planted, the pest control measures start. This plan can work well, but many times it involves using lots of chemicals to be effective. The question is, when is it necessary to step in with pest control measures? Take this short quiz to determine if you're overprotecting your garden.

~ Do you start spraying before you see any bugs?

~ When you see a bug, do you start every pest control measure you know and treat your whole garden?

~ When you find a bug, do you stop everything and check every plant in your garden?

~ Do you believe that most bugs in your garden are "bad guys"?

If you think that answering yes to most of these questions is pretty extreme, then you probably aren't overprotecting your garden. However, if you found yourself answering most of these questions in the affirmative, then you may need to pull back a little bit. Here are a few facts that may help you do that:

~ Over 95 percent of bugs found in your garden are either beneficial or do no harm at all.

~ Spot-treating plants that have pests is better than treating your whole garden.

~ Water is one of the most effective weapons against pests.

~ Over time, beneficial insects are likely to do just as good a job of controlling pest insects as spraying chemicals.

~ Ensuring that your plants are healthy and vigorous is the best preventative measure you can take for your garden.

Okay, you understand all of this. What should you do now?

~ Keep a garden log. Write down when and where you planted everything. List the dates when you saw bugs and on which plant. Next year, try planting later or earlier when the bugs aren't a problem. (It is good to keep a log for plant diseases too; in this case, write down when you first noted a plant disease starting.)

~ Know your enemy. If you have bugs in your garden, find out what they are. The same is true when it comes to plant diseases. Many books, such as field guides and gardening books, offer extensive insect identifications. There is usually someone on the staff at your local nursery who will know the local pests. The nearby university, natural history museum, or county extension office will also be able to help you identify insects. You may find that the bugs in your garden aren't doing anything harmful at all!

~ Use specific pest-control strategies in your garden. If you have aphids, don't treat your garden with *Bacillus thuringiensi* (Bt) for caterpillars, just in case. Bt is a bacterium used as an insecticide. There are more than thirty-five varieties, several of which are available to home gardeners. Bt (*kurstaki*) affects common pest caterpillars in the butterfly and moth family. It can also hurt beneficial caterpillars, so be careful when using it. Bt (*israelensi*) affects the larvae of blackflies, fungus gnats, and mosquitoes. Bt (*san diego*) affects certain leaf-feeding insects, such as black vine weevils, boll weevils, Colorado potato beetles, and elm leaf beetles. As with all pesticides, even those that are considered nontoxic to people, read the label carefully before using.

~ If you decide to bring in beneficial insects, make sure they are effective in your area.

~ Plan ahead when planting. Make sure the soil is in top condition before planting to ensure healthy plants.

~ Plant only plants that grow well in your area or are resistant to diseases found in your area.

~ Finally, decide how much damage you are willing to accept. Having an organic garden means finding a balance between the good bugs and the bad bugs. You must expect some insect damage. How much is too much for you?

You've done all this, yet find you still have too many holes in your lettuce leaves or aphids on your cabbages. Then it is time to start taking pest control measures.

~ First, identify the pest insect. Use sticky traps or collect the pest from the plant. Use field guides or take the insect to a nursery, university, or agricultural extension office for identification.

~ Select the pest control measure that will have the least effect on beneficial insects and the environment, such as using a trap that lures the pest away from your plants, or hand-picking. Hand-picking is a great solution for hornworm caterpillars, for example.

~ Spray only the affected plant. Soap spray is one example of a good control measure, but only spray where necessary.

~ Select a pest control measure that targets the pest. Use the insect's own biology against it. An insect cannot become resistant to its own biology, and you will win this battle every time. For example, use a bait for ants that you know they will carry back to their nest and feed to their young. This won't kill the ants right away, but if you are patient you will find that the whole mound will be dead in a week or two.

~ Use and encourage beneficial, natural controls. Plant composite flowers like daisies that have many small flowers packed tightly together to attract beneficial insects, or put out bird feeders that attract insect-eating birds.

~ Don't expect total eradication of pests. There are always new pests ready to step in.

ATTRACTING AND KEEPING BENEFICIAL INSECTS IN YOUR GARDEN

Beneficial insects are easy to attract and keep around if you provide them with the food and shelter they need. If you are attracting beneficial insects, it is very important that that you use no pesticides in your garden, or you will inadvertently kill the good insects along with the bad. Many beneficial insects are very small and you may never know they are in your garden; others are larger and always seem to be on patrol.

A general approach to attracting beneficial insects is to plant a few known host plants in and around your garden. Some favorites are dill, carrots, calendulas, zinnias, sunflowers, basil, thyme, sage, asters, yarrow, marigolds, parsley, and artemisia. Many other composite flowers that attract butterflies attract beneficial insects too. It is also a good idea to provide a water source, such as a birdbath or a saucer of water placed on the ground. Finally, try to control stray weeds around your garden that might harbor pest insects.

This section will help you address specific pest problems. It lists the most common beneficial insects, the insects they control, and what they need to take up permanent residence in your garden.

APHID MIDGE

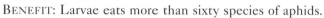

ADULTS: ⅟₁₆ (1.5 mm) inch long. Looks like
a very small wasp, but a very delicate one.
LARVAE OR CATERPILLARS: Small, ⅛-inch
orange maggot.
BENEFIT: Larvae eats more than sixty species of aphids.
RANGE: Throughout North America.
HOW TO ATTRACT: Landscape with plants that have plenty of pollen
and nectar in areas protected from the wind. Provide a water source.
NOTES: Available commercially. Adults are active mostly at night.

ASSASSIN BUG

ADULTS: ½ to 1⅜ inches long (12 to 33 mm). True bugs,
or insects in the order *Hemiptera*, that are flattened with
elongated heads. The beak is usually curved and tucks
under head into a groove. Some species are brightly colored, others not.
NYMPHS: Similar to adults but smaller.
BENEFIT: Predator of many common pest species of
insects, including flies and caterpillars.
RANGE: Throughout North America.
HOW TO ATTRACT: Assassin bugs are found naturally in
most gardens where insects are present.

BIG-EYED BUG

ADULTS: ⅛ to ¼ inch (3 to 6 mm) long. Fast-moving true bug with large eyes and minute black
spots on head and thorax.
NYMPHS: Similar to adults, but smaller and wingless.
BENEFIT: Eats aphids, leafhoppers, plant bugs,
spider mites, and small caterpillars.
RANGE: Western North America.
HOW TO ATTRACT: Big-eyed bugs are found mostly
in field crops and orchards. They like to lay their
eggs on soybeans, pigweed, and goldenrod. Small
weedy areas next to crops make a great shelter for these bugs.

BRACONID WASP

ADULTS: ⅒ to ½ inch (2.4 to 12 mm) long. Black
or brown with thin thread waists.

LARVAE OR CATERPILLARS: Very small, cream-colored
grubs that feed on other insects.

BENEFIT: Braconid wasps lay eggs that parasitize and kill
aphids, armyworms, cabbageworms, codling moths, corn borers,
elm bark beetles, hornworms, and some flies.

RANGE: Throughout North America.

HOW TO ATTRACT: Plant nectar plants such as dill, parsley, and yarrow
for the adults. Provide a water source.

NOTES: Available commercially.

BUMBLEBEE

ADULTS: ½ to 1 inch (12 to 24 mm) long. Plump, with
black and yellow striping on thorax, black face and head,
smoky-color wings, hairy body. Pollen basket on hind legs.

LARVAE: White grubs.

BENEFIT: Pollinators.

RANGE: Throughout North America.

HOW TO ATTRACT: Supply plenty of pollen and nectar flowers.
Bumblebees are naturally occurring in most gardens.

DAMSEL BUG

ADULTS: ⅜ to ½ inch (9 to 12 mm) long. Fast-
moving true bug with elongated gray or brown
body.

NYMPHS: Similar to adults but smaller and wingless.

BENEFIT: Nymphs are predators of aphids, leafhoppers, plant bugs, and thrips.

RANGE: Throughout North America.

HOW TO ATTRACT: Damsel bugs love alfalfa.

GROUND OR CARABID BEETLE

ADULTS: ¾ to 1 inch (18 to 24 mm) long. Beetles are black or brown
in color. Head, thorax, and abdomen are well defined, and on
many, iridescent.

LARVAE: Dark brown or black grubs that have ten segments. Body ta-
pers toward the abdomen tip.

BENEFIT: Large group of beetles that are predators of cabbageworms, cutworms, slugs, snails, and most ground insects. Larvae are also predators with giant appetites.

RANGE. Throughout North America.

HOW TO ATTRACT: These beetles are naturally occurring in most gardens. Provide shelter for them by planting permanent beds or adding stones near the garden they can crawl under. Paths throughout the garden that are planted with white clover, sod, or a ground cover are suitable to shelter as well.

HONEYBEE

ADULTS: Female worker bees are ⅜ to ⅝ inch (9 to 15 mm) long. Males are a bit larger with larger eyes. Gold- and black-striped hairy body; translucent wings.

LARVAE: White grubs found in their hives.

BENEFIT: Pollinators.

RANGE. Worldwide.

HOW TO ATTRACT: Provide pollen and nectar plants. Provide a water source.

NOTES: Average size of hive is 60,000 to 80,000 bees.

HOVER FLY (FLOWER FLY)

ADULTS. ½ to ⅝ inch (12 to 15 mm) long. Resemble honeybees when hovering over flowers. Abdomen flattened with yellow or white and black striping. Two translucent wings.

BENEFIT: Larvae feed on aphids, mealybugs, and other small insects.

RANGE: Throughout North America.

HOW TO ATTRACT: Landscape with plants that have a lot of pollen and nectar. Plant yarrow or composite flowers among garden plants to attract the adults.

ICHNEUMON WASP

ADULTS: ⅛ to 3 inches (3 to 72 mm) long. Take many colors but the most common are brown and black. Bodies are slender. Females often have a very long ovipositor that people may misperceive as a stinger. All have long antennae that are in constant motion.

LARVAE: Small grubs with tapered ends.

BENEFIT: Adults feed on many different types of insects and spiders. Adult females parasitize caterpillars and then lay eggs on the caterpillars that in turn feed on the caterpillars.

RANGE: Throughout North America.

HOW TO ATTRACT: Landscape with plants rich in pollen and nectar. Females especially like flowering clover. Provide a water source.

LACEWING

ADULTS: ½ to ¾ inch (12 to 18 mm) long. Two types are most common: green-colored lacewings and brown-colored lacewings. Large, netlike transparent wings form a tent over the abdomen when at rest. Head is small with large eyes.

LARVAE: Spindle-shaped body is usually mottled yellow or brown.

BENEFIT: Both larvae and adults are predators of aphids, mealybugs, and many other small soft insects. Larva called the "aphid lion."

RANGE: Throughout North America.

HOW TO ATTRACT: Allow some flowering composite plants—carrots and dill, for example—to grow and flower in the garden. Plant flowers that have lots of pollen and nectar, and provide a water source.

NOTES: Sold commercially. Eggs laid on long stalks on underside of leaves.

LADYBUG (LADYBIRD BEETLE)

ADULTS: ⅟₁₆ to ⅜ inch (1.5 to 9 mm) long. Bodies are round and often spotted. Most are shiny red, orange, or yellow in color with black markings.

LARVAE: Spindle-shaped body is covered with spines, bright spots, and bands.

BENEFIT: Both larvae and adults feed on aphids, scales, mealybugs, and small insects.

RANGE: Worldwide.

HOW TO ATTRACT: Landscape with plants rich in pollen and nectar-producing flowers. Plant carrots, yarrow, or another composite flower in the garden and allow to bloom.

NOTES: Available commercially. Mexican bean beetles are also a member of this group and are not considered beneficial.

MEALYBUG DESTROYER

ADULTS: ⅓ inch (8 to 9 mm) long. Body is oval, wing covers are black. Head and tip of abdomen is coral-colored.

LARVAE: Cream-colored larvae with lots of long, waxy filaments all over body.

BENEFIT: Both larvae and adults feed on mealybugs.

RANGE: Western coastal regions of North America.

HOW TO ATTRACT: Occur naturally in native areas when mealybugs are present.

NOTES: Sold commercially.

MINUTE PIRATE BUG

ADULTS: ¼ inch (6 mm) long. Quick-moving true bugs with a black and white pattern.

NYMPHS: Similar to adults but wingless. Nymphs go through many color changes—from yellow to orange to brown—before reaching their adult coloration.

BENEFIT: Predators of thrips, spider mites, small caterpillars, immature leafhoppers, and insect eggs.

RANGE: Throughout North America.

HOW TO ATTRACT: Plant goldenrod, daisies, yarrow, alfalfa, and other flowering plants that produce pollen and nectar.

NOTES: Sold commercially. Average release rate is one pirate bug for up to five plants.

NEMATODE

ADULTS: ⅕₅ inch to several inches (.96 to 72 mm) long for beneficial nematodes. Many others are microscopic. Over 10,000 species, with some categorized as pests.

BENEFIT: Parasitic nematodes attack and parasitize many soil-dwelling immature insects such as fleas, root weevils, crown borers, corn rootworms, and grubs of many beetle species.

RANGE: Throughout North America.

HOW TO ATTRACT: Naturally occurring in moist soils. To increase populations, purchase commercially sold nematodes and add to moist soil.

NOTES: Sold commercially.

PRAYING MANTIS

ADULTS: 2 to 2½ inches (48 to 60 mm) long.
  Large green or tan insects with big compound
  eyes. Wings extend beyond abdomen. Large front legs to
  catch insects.

NYMPHS: Similar to adults but smaller.

BENEFIT: Predators of almost all insects. Unfortunately, these indiscriminate eaters will devour beneficial insects as well.

RANGE: Southern and eastern United States into Ontario. Another species of mantis lives in the West.

HOW TO ATTRACT: Provide permanent plantings for mantises to overwinter near the garden.

NOTES: Sold commercially.

PREDATORY MITE

ADULTS: Minute fast-moving mites. Colors range
  from beige to reddish brown.

NYMPHS: Similar to adults but smaller.

BENEFIT: Predators of spider mites, European red
  mites, citrus red mites, other mite species, and
  thrips.

RANGE: Throughout North America.

HOW TO ATTRACT: Naturally occurring populations.
  To maintain native species of predatory mites or
  increase their numbers, sprinkle pollen from ice plants, cattails, or
  dandelions on plants.

NOTES: Sold commercially.

SNAKEFLY

ADULTS: ½ to 1 inch (12 to 24 mm) long. Dark insects
  with pronounced head that can be raised, unlike most insects.
  Wings are transparent and have netlike veining. Wings are folded,
  tentlike, when at rest over the body.

LARVAE: Black bodies; they look very similar to beetle larvae.

BENEFIT: Both the larvae and adults are active predators on other insects such as aphids and caterpillars.

RANGE: Mostly in the western United States and British Columbia.

HOW TO ATTRACT: Occur naturally in native areas; always looking
  for prey.

SOLDIER BEETLE

ADULTS: ⅓ to ½ inch (8 to 12 mm) long. Long,
slender beetles that are flattened. Wing covers are
leathery and appear downy. Pronounced head
and thorax.

LARVAE: Dark, flattened grubs that are covered
with hairs.

BENEFIT: Both larvae and adults are predators of aphids,
cucumber beetles, corn rootworms, grasshopper eggs, caterpillars,
and beetle larvae.

RANGE: Throughout North America.

HOW TO ATTRACT: To attract adults, plant goldenrod, milkweed, hydrangeas, or catnip. Larvae overwinter in the soil, so keep some
permanent plantings for the beetles to have a place to lay their eggs.

SPINED SOLDIER BUG

ADULTS: ½ inch (12 mm) long. True bugs that are
grayish brown and shield-shaped. Shoulders of thorax
come to sharp points.

NYMPHS: Similar to adults but wingless.

BENEFIT: Predator of caterpillars, grubs, armyworms,
sawflies, and Mexican bean beetle larvae.

RANGE: Throughout North America.

HOW TO ATTRACT: Provide shelter of permanent perennial plants
near the garden.

TACHINID FLY

ADULTS: ⅓ to ½ inch (8 to 12 mm) long. Gray,
brown, or black. Look like big hairy houseflies
with mottled colored bodies.

LARVAE: Cream to whitish-color maggots.

BENEFIT: Females deposit eggs that parasitize and kill caterpillars of
many pest species, such as cabbage loopers, gypsy moths, armyworms, and tent caterpillars.

RANGE: Throughout North America.

HOW TO ATTRACT: Adult flies feed on flower nectar. Plant such flowers as dill, parsley, and sweet clover. Watch for caterpillars with
white eggs attached to them, and don't kill the caterpillars. These
eggs will eventually turn into more tachinid flies.

TIGER BEETLES

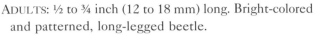

ADULTS: ½ to ¾ inch (12 to 18 mm) long. Bright-colored and patterned, long-legged beetle.

LARVAE: S-shaped, segmented grubs have a hump on the fifth segment. The hump is covered with strong hooks.

BENEFIT: Both the larvae and the adults feed on other insect species.

RANGE: Throughout North America.

HOW TO ATTRACT: Provide shelter by planting permanent perennial plants near the garden.

NOTES: Beetles are often drawn to lights at night.

HOW TO BUY BENEFICIAL INSECTS

You've determined that you need the help of beneficial insects and you would like to purchase some for your garden. How do you find the right supplier?

BUYING INSECT HELP

You can purchase beneficial insects in several different ways. Many nurseries and home centers now carry them during the spring and summer months. They usually have adult ladybugs and parasitic nematodes, and sometimes even praying mantis eggs. The selection varies widely.

Your local nursery is the best source for parasitic nematodes. They come suspended in a clay base for retail sale; the nematodes last longer on the shelf than live insects do. Still, always check the expiration date on the package to make sure the nematodes are not left over from last year.

Some nurseries don't carry live insects at all, but instead sell you an order form that you mail in. The insects then arrive at your home in about a week.

Your best bet for buying live insects is to order them directly from the supplier. Usually you can save yourself some money. Check the buying guide at the back of this book for supplier names and addresses.

Decide which insects you are interested in buying, and then do some calling around. Many suppliers have a toll-free number; use it. Be sure to ask a few questions. Here are some examples:

- How much do the insects cost, and how many do you get for the price? Prices vary.

- If you are not sure about a certain insect surviving in your area, ask if it will survive in your climate and for how long. The supplier may know of another insect that will do the job better.

- Does the supplier guarantee the insects will be delivered live? Things can happen in shipment. Look for a return policy in case they arrive dead.

- In what form will the insects arrive? Eggs, pupae, adults?

- Will instructions be included in the package concerning handling, rearing of eggs or pupae, and the best way to release the insects?

- Is this a good time of year to release the insects into the garden or is there a better time?

- Is the supplier a member of the Association of Natural Biocontrol Producers? Members are generally reputable and will try hard to make sure their customers are satisfied.

WHAT TO DO WITH THE CRITTERS

Once the insects arrive at your home, follow the instructions that come with them precisely. Some live insect adults are shipped on ice to keep them cool and slow down their systems. They should start moving around in about thirty minutes after being taken off the ice.

It is very discouraging to release ladybugs or other adult beneficial insects, only to see them all fly away. Try this trick to keep them around long enough to eat some of your pests (of course, do this only if there are no specific releasing instructions from the supplier): Wet the pest-infested plants well and release the insects on them in the evening. Generally, ladybugs are thirsty when released and immediately look for water. If the foliage is wet, they may stop for a drink and then decide to stay the night. In the morning, they will be right where you want them, ready to eat the pests you want to get rid of.

INSECT-KILLING SPRAYS AND METHODS

You can easily make your own insect-killing sprays and repellents, many of them with ingredients that come straight out of your kitchen cupboard or medicine chest. These sprays and repellents are just as effective and a lot less toxic to the environment than those that are available commercially. In fact, many are completely nontoxic.

Remember, as with any spray, always test these first. Spray a couple of leaves and then check the leaves in a day or two for burning. If there isn't any burning, then it is safe to spray the whole plant.

HORTICULTURAL OIL SPRAYS

Horticultural oil sprays have been commercially available for quite some time. They work by smothering the insects and mites they come in contact with, thus preventing several disease-causing pests from taking up residency on such favored plants as roses, hydrangeas, phlox, and zinnias. When oil is mixed with other ingredients it can also kill fungal diseases that are present on the plant.

Aphids, scale insects, and other insects that stay on the plant are particularly susceptible to oil. In contrast, grasshoppers and insects that take a bite and leave quickly are not usually affected. When using any spray, remember that it will kill beneficial insects as well as pests and spray only when you are sure the pests are present. Also, oils can burn sensitive plants, especially during hot summer months, so before spraying an entire plant always spray a few leaves and then check the next day for burning. Cauliflower, red cabbage, and squash are very susceptible to oil burning. Special so-called *summer oils* are commercially available. They are very light and evaporate off the plant quickly.

For best results, spray both the upper and undersides of the leaves when the temperature is between 40 and 90 degrees.

If you make your own oil spray, you can tailor it to your specific needs. Here are a few simple recipes.

Basic oil spray

Step 1: Make the oil mixture

1 cup vegetable oil (safflower, corn, soybean, or canola)
1 tablespoon dishwashing liquid

Place oil and water in a jar or empty plastic ketchup bottle. Squeezable ketchup bottles make for easy pouring and measuring. Leftovers can be kept in these containers for later use.

Step 2: Make the spray

1 tablespoon oil mixture from Step 1
(for delicate plants reduce the oil mixture to 1 teaspoon)
2 cups water

Place the solution in sprayer or spray bottle, and spray plant. Because oil and water don't mix well, shake sprayer bottle periodically while treating to keep the solution well mixed. Repeat treatment in seven to ten days if necessary.

Alcohol oil spray

To increase the effectiveness of the basic oil spray, add some isopropyl alcohol to the mixture. An alcohol and water solution is lethal to many insects.

1 cup alcohol
1 teaspoon vegetable oil
1 quart water

Mix ingredients together and place in spray bottle. Spray on pest-infested plants as necessary.

Garlic oil spray

Garlic is a bug-busting wonder. It can repel and—when mixed with oil—kill some of the biggest garden pests, including aphids, cabbage moths, cabbage loopers, earwigs, leafhoppers, mosquitoes, and whiteflies. Besides working on insects, garlic also kills the harmful fungi that cause plant diseases like powdery mildew, rust, and gray mold. (See page 24 for details.)

Step 1: Make the garlic oil

> *1 whole head of garlic, minced (or run through a garlic press)*
> *1 cup vegetable oil*

Mix garlic and oil together. Let the mixture sit for up to two days in the refrigerator. (Fresh garlic and oil will turn rancid if not refrigerated.) The oil should have a strong garlic smell when ready. If it doesn't, add more garlic and let sit another day. Strain out garlic.

Step 2: Make the spray

> *2 to 3 teaspoons garlic oil (see Step 1)*
> *1 quart water*
> *2 to 3 drops dishwashing liquid*

Spray plants when insects appear or at first signs of mildew. Repeat treatment in two weeks if necessary.

Dormant tree oil spray

Use dormant tree oil spray to protect your stone fruit trees— apricots, peaches, and plums, for example—against both insects and fungus. This is a two-part procedure for dormant trees only. First, spray the tree with copper sulfate. Copper sulfate is available at all nurseries. Wait a few days for the copper sulfate to dry completely. Second, make the following mixture.

> *1 gallon water*
> *12 tablespoons canola or safflower oil*
> *1 teaspoon dishwashing liquid*

Pour into sprayer and spray entire tree.

OTHER HOMEMADE INSECT-KILLING SPRAYS

Here are a few other insect-killing sprays that can be made with ordinary household items.

Basic soap spray

Soap spray is probably the most common of all homemade sprays. It works best on soft-bodied insects such as mites, aphids, whiteflies, thrips, and many other insects in their immature stages. It works by penetrating the cell membranes and causing the insects to dry out. Soap is less effective on fast-moving insects, because the spray must come into contact with them. With insects that have very tough coverings, you may need additional soap spray treatments to kill them completely. Soap is safe on edible vegetables and usually leaves no residue on plants.

> 2 tablespoons dishwashing liquid
> 1 gallon warm water

Mix and use as a spray. Repeat as necessary.

Extra-easy soap spray

Place a bar of soap in the toe of an old pantyhose leg. Tie the pantyhose to the handle of watering can, so the bar of soap hangs inside. Fill the can with warm water and swish the bar around for a few seconds, or let sit for a minute. Use this soapy water on your plants. Experiment with the time you let the bar sit in the water. Start with a few seconds and increase the time until you achieve the right concentration to kill the pests—different soaps may need different lengths of time to dissolve. When finished watering, just let the soap in the pantyhose hang inside the can until dry. Repeat as necessary.

Other ingredients may be added to the basic soap spray for greater effectiveness.

- ~ Add sulfur to kill mites, fungi, and insects; see package directions for amounts.
- ~ Add 1 or 2 tablespoons of baking soda to the basic soap recipe and you will kill fungi as well as insects.

~ Add citrus oils (1 or 2 teaspoons) for extra penetrating power.

~ The caffeine in coffee and tea has been shown to disrupt the behavior of many insects. When added to an insecticide, coffee and tea increase its effectiveness. Instead of pouring that stale old brew out when you make a new pot, save it and replace some of the water in your favorite soap recipe with a cup or two.

~ Finally, peppermint mixed with soap is very effective at cutting through the waxy defenses of many insects. Mix 1 or 2 teaspoons of peppermint extract into your soap recipe, or use a commercially purchased liquid peppermint soap to make your soap spray.

Lemon spray

Here's one more use for the handy lemon: it can be made into quite an effective insect spray. The chemical *limonene*, found in lemon peels, is an effective killing agent. Whiteflies and soft-bodied insects are killed quickly with this spray. It can even get rid of fleas on your pet. However, just like people, pets can be allergic to lemons. To use as a flea killer, sponge mixture on pet. Then leave it on, or rinse it off. If shaking or signs of an allergic reaction start, shampoo pet immediately. If symptoms persist, call your veterinarian.

Peels of 2 large or 4 small lemons

1 quart water

Boil the lemon peels for 10 minutes. Cool. Take out peels, and place solution in a spray bottle.

Ammonia spray for mites

Mites can be a big problem for many plant species. Those of us who grow fuchsias know that mites on these beautiful plants can be hard to fight. This spray not only kills the mites but also acts as a mild fertilizer.

2½ gallons water

1 teaspoon dishwashing liquid

3 teaspoons ammonia

Mix solution and pour into spray bottle. Treat plants every five days for three weeks to get rid of mites.

Diatomaceous earth

Diatomaceous earth (DE) is the fossilized shells of microscopic sea diatoms, which act like tiny razor blades on insects. When an insect comes in contact with DE, it is injured and eventually dries out and dies. DE comes in two grades, garden grade and swimming-pool grade. When treating plants, be sure to use only garden-grade DE. The swimming-pool grade is much coarser and is not intended for garden use.

Dusting plants with DE prevents many chewing and sucking insects from harming them. Mist the plant with water first and then lightly dust on the DE. The mist helps hold the DE in place. Dust as much of the plant as possible. A note of caution: always wear a dust mask when using any fine dusting material.

If you find dusting too tedious, you can make a DE spray.

Diatomaceous earth spray

1 quart water
1 teaspoon liquid insecticidal soap or dishwashing liquid
¼ pound DE

Mix ingredients together and place in a 5-gallon sprayer. Add more water to fill. Shake to mix. Spray plants.

You can use DE in other ways as well. To stop snail and slug damage to plants, ring the plants with DE. This works to prevent damage from crawling caterpillars on young trees as well.

Sowbugs also are very vulnerable to DE. Make a paste from DE and water and spread it on the trucks of trees. Again, this will control caterpillars as well.

Sprinkle DE around seedlings to help protect them from hungry grubs and maggots. Also, if you dust seeds with DE either before planting or when they are on the ground, they will stand a better chance against weevils and other seed-eating insects.

DE washes off with water. Reapply after rainstorms or overhead-watering for maximum effectiveness.

Flour spray

Our grandparents knew that dusting a plant with flour was a good way to kill many pest insects. The flour dust turns into a sticky substance that can hold a pest like a sticky trap. Or the insects eat it, and the flour stops up their digestive tracts. To get more flour on the plant try spraying it on.

2 to 4 tablespoons wheat or potato flour
½ teaspoon dishwashing liquid
1 quart water

Mix ingredients well and place in spray bottle. Spray on plant leaves and stems.

INSECT REPELLENTS

These common foods and plants repel many types of insects; some are all-purpose, others are insect-specific.

ALL-PURPOSE REPELLENTS

Anise

Anise is a good repellent for a variety of pests. Many gardeners report less of a problem with aphids, fleas, and cabbage pests when anise is planted nearby.

Catnip

Catnip deters many pests, such as Colorado potato beetles, darkling beetles, flea beetles, Japanese beetles, squash bugs, weevils, and probably the biggest pest of all, ants. However, when planting catnip understand that your garden will be a favorite stop for every cat in the neighborhood.

Garlic

Garlic has been known to repel not only insects but animals as well. Plant edible garlic between vegetable rows or next to roses to repel aphids and many other insects. Garlic powder can be dusted directly on the plant, or garlic can be made into a spray for a more concentrated dose. Try one of the following garlic sprays.

All-purpose garlic spray

> 6 cloves garlic
> ½ onion
> 1 tablespoon cayenne pepper
> 1 tablespoon dishwashing liquid
> 1 quart water

Put first four ingredients into a blender, add some of the water, and blend until smooth. Pour mixture into a jar and add the rest of the water. Let steep for 24 hours. Strain, then pour the liquid into a spray bottle. Treat plants. Keep extra spray in refrigerator for up to 2 weeks. Treat again if necessary.

Easy garlic spray

> ½ cup finely chopped garlic cloves
>   (onion or chives may be substituted for garlic)
> 1 pint water

Mix garlic and water well. Let sit for about an hour. Strain out garlic and pour into spray bottle. Treat plants with fine mist.

Geraniums

Geraniums have long been noted for their resistance to pests. It is thought that their often pungent odor repels insects. Rose growers have noted that when they plant white geraniums among and around their rose bushes they have fewer problems with Japanese beetles. Gardeners have noted fewer pests when scented geraniums are planted near tomatoes. Make a geranium spray to use on plants to repel many kinds of insects. (This recipe may also be made with marigolds or any pungent plant, including garlic.)

Geranium repellent spray

Combine equal amounts of geraniums and water in a blender, and whirl until smooth. Strain mixture through a cheesecloth or fine strainer. To use, dilute the geranium liquid at the rate of 1 teaspoon to 2 cups water. Spray where needed.

Hot peppers

Many people claim that hot pepper plants provide some repellent qualities when planted in among other plants. Some say hot peppers keep down the occurrence of black spot. Try making your own hot pepper spray. Just remember to wash off any vegetables you spray with this mixture before eating them.

Hot pepper repellent spray

*3 to 4 hot peppers (serrano, habanero,
or other very hot pepper), chopped*

1 quart boiling water

1 quart cold water

2 drops dishwashing liquid (optional)

Drop peppers into a pot of boiling water. Remove pot from the stove and let steep for 24 hours. Discard peppers. Add the cold water to dilute the pepper solution. Add the dishwashing liquid to help the spray stick to the plant. Be sure to check a small spot on your plant for burning before spraying the entire plant.

Hot peppers that have been made into powders like chili powder, cayenne pepper, black pepper, and red pepper can also be made into pepper sprays or used alone. The ingredient that makes them hot, *capsaicin,* is known to repel lots of insects, from ants to root maggots. Ring vulnerable seedlings of onions, cabbages, carrots, or other plants with hot pepper powder to protect them. Dust it on plants to control caterpillars, too. It's a good idea to wear a dust mask when using hot pepper powder. And keep it away from pets. Of course, if your pets are bothering your garden, this just might keep them out! Generally dogs don't like the smell of pepper.

Marigolds

The beautiful marigold flower provides a garden not only with great color but with insect-repelling qualities as well. Some of the pests it repels are Mexican bean beetles, asparagus beetles, tomato hornworms, and many cabbage pests. Gardeners plant marigolds next to cabbages, potatoes, and tomatoes. Scientists have shown that, planted within a three-foot radius of vegetables, marigolds actually keep nematodes in the soil away as well. You can make an insect-repellent spray with marigolds by following the recipe for the geranium spray on page 59, but substitute marigolds for geraniums.

Nasturtiums

Nasturtiums planted among other plants have been shown to repel many different kinds of insects, such as aphids, cabbage loopers, squash bugs, and whiteflies. One attractive way to do this is to plant nasturtiums with vining crops such as squash, cucumbers, and melons. Potatoes planted next to nasturtiums are said to have fewer problems with potato beetles. An extra bonus to using nasturtiums is that the flowers are edible! Try adding them to your next tossed salad.

Petunias

Petunias look pretty in your garden, but studies have shown they also actually repel a number of pests, including Mexican bean beetles, potato bugs, and squash bugs.

Rosemary

Rosemary is known to repel Mexican bean beetles, cabbage moths, and carrot flies.

Tansy

Tansy has been known for quite some time to be a great repellent for many different types of insect pests. Many gardeners swear that tansy planted in a ring around their fruit trees helps to repel fruit flies. Tansy is also said to repel Japanese beetles, ants, aphids, cabbage loopers, squash bugs, and beetles.

Tomatoes

Perhaps you have noticed that very few pests bother tomatoes. Tomato plants contain alkaloids that repel many insects, including cabbage pests, asparagus and flea beetles, and whiteflies. Often tomatoes are planted with beans, cabbage, onions, and peas to protect these crops from pests. Try making this solution from tomato leaves to spray on other plants to repel pests.

Tomato leaf spray

2 cups chopped tomato leaves
1 quart water
½ teaspoon dishwashing liquid

Combine the tomato leaves and water in a saucepan. Heat to simmering, then turn off the heat. Let mixture steep until cool. Strain the leaves from the water and add soap to the water. Place solution in sprayer or spray bottle and use where needed. The solution should have a "tomatoey" smell. Spray where needed.

INSECT-SPECIFIC REPELLENTS

Try using these natural repellents for specific pests.

~ Banana peels placed around roses and other plants plagued by aphids will make the pests disappear. How banana peels repel aphids is still unclear, but it seems to work. Keep putting the peels around the base of the plants as long as aphids are a problem. As a bonus, the potassium in the peels stimulates larger blooms.

~ Citrus rinds have a chemical in them that deters corn earworms. To make a solution of citrus rinds, chop up the rinds of 2 to 4 fruits. Place them in a container with a quart of hot water. Let sit overnight. Strain out rinds and spray on affected plants. Another easy lemon spray is on page 56.

~ Lemongrass repels wasps. Wasps can be quite annoying at a picnic or barbecue. Next time, take along some lemongrass and lay it on the picnic table or put it in a vase. The wasps will stay away.

~ Peppermint tea sprayed onto plants has been shown to repel Colorado potato beetles. Steep two peppermint tea bags or about ¼ cup fresh chopped mint leaves in a quart of very hot water for thirty minutes. Let the tea cool, then strain and spray on plants. Experiment with the strength of the spray. And try it on other plants for other pest problems. Research shows that mint may be a good all-purpose repellent.

~ Old tires used as planters repel squash and cucumber beetles. In addition, many gardeners have had good success planting heat-loving plants inside old tires.

~ Wood ashes are a way to get rid of cucumber beetles. Make a spray out of wood ashes by mixing ½ cup ashes in 2 gallons of water. Put solution in watering can and water plants. Note that if mildew or other fungi are a problem, overhead watering is not advised. Furthermore, ashes are very alkaline, so use sparingly on alkaline soils.

COMPANION PLANTINGS TO REPEL SPECIFIC INSECTS

By planting certain crops together, you will repel insects on your favored crop.

~ Borage repels Japanese beetles on potatoes. Borage also is a great plant for attracting many beneficial insects.

~ Chrysanthemums planted in soils that have nematode problems have reduced the populations of nematodes.

~ Dead nettle or henbit, a member of the mint family, is believed to repel potato bugs. Just plant it among your other plants. Many gardeners report that dead nettle also improves the growth and flavor of many vegetables when planted together with them.

~ Dill planted in the garden is a great general repellent for aphids and spider mites.

·- Fennel is said to repel aphids in the garden when planted near susceptible plants.

~ Green beans planted with eggplants repel Colorado potato beetles.

~ Leeks planted with carrots repel carrot flies.

~ Mint planted next to broccoli and cauliflower is said to repel cabbage loopers, which love the taste of nice fresh heads. Although it's a wonderful garden addition, mint can become invasive. Here's an easy solution: Cut the top and bottom rounds from a large coffee can. Then "plant" the can in the garden with the open lip at soil level, and plant the mint inside the buried can.

~ Onions planted with cabbage, carrot, corn, potatoes, and tomatoes show some ability to repel several pest insects, including potato beetles and carrot flies.

~ Parsley planted with carrots repels carrot worms. As an added benefit, you can harvest the parsley to use fresh or dried.

~ Potatoes planted near beans, cabbage, cauliflower, and corn have been shown to repel attacks from Mexican bean beetles.

~ Radishes planted around cucumbers, cabbages, melons, and other vegetables are said to repel many insects, including cucumber beetles, root flies, and vine borers.

~ Sage repels cabbage flies and root maggots. When planting members of the cabbage family like broccoli or cauliflower, try planting some sage around them. Sage works well to repel pest insects from carrots, too.

~ Thyme has been shown to repel cabbage loopers and whiteflies when planted near cabbage plants.

INSECT TRAPS

Insect traps can go a long way in keeping numbers of certain insects down and preventing plant damage. The idea is to attract the insects to something they like and keep them off what you like. Many different kinds of traps can help you grow beautiful plants and vegetables for yourself, not for the pests.

HOMEMADE TRAPS

With one of us an entomologist and the other a gardener, we have heard about every kind of insect trap known to humankind. Many of our readers have kindly sent us their tried-and-true insect-trap ideas. Some of those they've told us about use bait to lure the insects, others are more inventive. We hope one helps you solve your insect problem.

Aphids (winged adults)

Adult aphids are attracted to yellow when migrating to other plants. It is thought that the insects perceive yellow as a patch of bright foliage. Make yellow sticky traps from heavy paper (see page 67 for details), purchase yellow sticky traps, or fill yellow buckets with water to attract and drown them.

Apple maggots, cherry fruit flies

Apple maggots and cherry fruit flies like red sticky sphere-shaped traps; walnut husk flies like green-colored ones. Make these traps by painting old balls or lightbulbs and then spraying them with spray adhesive. Hang them. When they are covered with flies throw them away. Or place red balls inside a plastic sandwich bag, and use a twist-tie to close the bag tightly over the ball. Now coat the plastic bag with a sticky substance, such as Tanglefoot. Hang a couple in each tree. When the ball is covered with insects, merely take the plastic off, discard, and repeat with another plastic bag. You can also trap apple maggots in jars or cans filled with a solution made of 1 part molasses and 9 parts water. Hang jars or cans in trees. The insects are attracted to the solution, fall in the cans, and drown.

Beetles

To make a trap for beetles, cut the top off a 1-gallon plastic milk jug, leaving the handle on. Fill the jug with water, and add a squirt of dishwashing liquid. When you see beetles feeding on your favorite plants, just slip the jug under the plant or branch and give the branch a quick tap. The beetles will fall into the jug and drown. Try this early in the morning when fast-moving beetles are still cold. This is a great method for trapping Japanese beetles because the creatures play dead when disturbed and don't try to fly away.

Clothes moths

To catch clothes moths, make a yellow sticky trap (see page 67) but put the adhesive on one side only. Then place some fish meal (fish food, purchased at a pet store) in the middle of the trap. Now place the trap on the floor of your closet. Another way to do this is with duct tape. Place the tape sticky side up on a piece of cardboard, and then put some fish meal in the center. Try the yellow trap and then the gray duct tape one to see if the color makes a difference. (Some say it does, others say it doesn't.) This trap will also catch dermestid beetles, silverfish, booklice, roaches, and crickets.

Codling moths

Wrap the trunk of your tree with corrugated paper or cardboard. This traps the small caterpillars before they climb up the tree to feed on its leaves. Replace paper periodically.

Cucumber beetles

To trap cucumber beetles, set out cantaloupe or cucumber rinds on a piece of newspaper. When you see beetles on the rinds, quickly crumble the paper to catch the beetles inside. Then dunk the paper with rinds and beetles in a large bucket of soapy water. Later, throw paper, rinds, and dead beetles right into the compost pile.

Cutworms

For cutworms in the soil, mix 1 gallon water with 3 tablespoons dishwashing liquid. Pour on trouble spot. The solution will bring the worms to the surface where you can invite birds to eat them or dispose of them yourself. For cutworms in the garden, lay boards around areas that have cutworms. Check under the boards during the day and discard coiled cutworms.

Earwigs

Here are two methods to catch earwigs. First: Lay six- to eight-inch pieces of old garden hose in places where earwigs are a problem. Then leave them there for a day or so. After that, shake the hose pieces over a bucket of soapy water to dislodge the earwigs from inside. Repeat. Second: Place a damp rolled-up newspaper in the garden in the evening. Pick up the paper with earwigs in the morning.

Flea beetles

Flea beetles are attracted to the color white. Try making white sticky traps. (See page 68 for details.) Flea beetles are also attracted to beer. Place a wide-mouthed jar containing one or two inches of beer in your garden. The beetles will fly in and drown.

Flies

To trap flies, mix 2 cups water with ½ cup sugar and ½ cup vinegar or apple cider vinegar. Place the solution in an empty two-liter soda bottle and set it outside. The flies will fly into the bottle and drown. To keep flies out of your house, take a large clear plastic bag and drop a small piece of aluminum foil in it. Then fill bag with water, tie it closed, and hang it over a window or doorway. Flies will no longer enter. Why? We aren't sure!

Fruit flies

Fruit flies are attracted to the color yellow, so make yellow traps to catch them. To make a yellow sticky trap, glue yellow paper to a piece of cardboard. Spray the paper with adhesive. Then hang or stake the paper outside to catch flies in the garden. A second way to make a sticky trap is to spray a piece of yellow plastic with cooking oil or rub petroleum jelly on it before hanging. Finally, you can use a yellow plastic bucket to make a lure. Just fill the bucket halfway with water and set it in the garden. Flies will be attracted to it and fall in and drown.

Grasshoppers

To trap grasshoppers, bury a sixteen-ounce coffee can up to its lip in or near your garden. Then fill the can almost to the top with a solution made up of 1 part molasses and 9 parts water. Grasshoppers are attracted to it and fall in and drown. Several other pest insects will be attracted as well.

Gypsy moths

Adult moths usually lay their eggs on tree trunks. When the caterpillars hatch, they crawl up the tree to feed. To catch them before they do, make a collar out of burlap. Take about two feet of burlap and tape it onto the trunk about two feet up off the ground. The burlap must wrap all around the trunk, like a sash, with a bit extra at the ends to overlap. Tie a string or cord around the middle of the sash. Then remove the tape and fold the upper portion down over the cord and lower portion. When caterpillars try to crawl up the tree, they will get caught in the fold. Check and remove caterpillars daily.

Hornworms

Hornworms are hard to spot because they blend in with the surrounding plants. Try spraying your plants with cold water. The hornworms will move about, making them easier to see and hand-pick.

Leafhoppers and leaf miners

Like fruit flies, leafhoppers and leaf miners are attracted to yellow sticky traps. (See above, under "Fruit flies," for details on making traps.)

Mosquitoes

Use the carnivorous sundew plant as a natural trap for mosquitoes. The plant has sticky stems. Hang the plant outside and it will catch many mosquitoes.

Rose chafers

Rose chafers are attracted to white, so make white sticky traps to catch them. Glue white paper to a piece of cardboard, then spray with adhesive. Now stake the paper traps among your rose bushes. (You can also purchase white sticky traps.)

Silverfish

To trap silverfish, take a small glass jar—a baby food jar, for example—and wrap the outside of it with masking tape (the sticky side facing in, sticking to the jar). Then put a little wheat flour into the jar as bait. Place jars under sinks or anywhere silverfish are present. The silverfish can climb the rough tape to get into the jar, but they can't climb back out on the slippery glass. Check often.

Slugs and snails

Here are two ways to trap slugs and snails. First: Lay a board out along the edges of your garden, propping one corner up just a bit. Slugs and snails will crawl under the board during the day seeking shade. Pick up the board and dispose of the creatures. Second: Place hollowed-out orange or melon rinds, cut side down, in your garden in the evenings. In the morning, just pick up the rinds and throw the slugs and snails away.

Sowbugs and pillbugs

To trap sowbugs or pillbugs, simply place cabbage or potato peels under a clay flowerpot in your garden. Every few days, harvest the bugs that have congregated under the pot. Then either place them elsewhere in your yard, such as the compost pile where they can work as decomposers, or dump them into a bucket of soapy water.

Tarnished plant bugs

Tarnished plant bugs are attracted to the color white, just as rose chafers are. Try making white sticky traps for them too.

Thrips

Thrips are attracted to blue and sometimes to yellow. Make sticky traps to catch them.

Wasps

Make a wasp trap from an empty two-liter soda bottle. The simplest method is to pour fruit punch or flat soda into the bottle (don't fill it more than halfway), leave the top off, and set the bottle outside. Wasps fly into the bottle, get caught in the liquid, and drown. But remember: wasps are actually beneficial insects and control many unwanted insects.

Whiteflies
Whiteflies are attracted to yellow sticky traps. (See page 67 for details.)

Wireworms
Trap wireworms in pieces of cut fresh potatoes scattered around the garden. Check potatoes daily for the worms and replace the potatoes with fresh ones as needed. Drop infested potatoes in a bucket of soapy water, then compost.

MULCH TRAPS
Many fruit tree pests—like cherry fruit flies, green fig beetles (June beetles), and Japanese beetles—lay their eggs in the soil under their favorite tree or shrub. To stop the larvae from emerging, lay plastic or a heavy mulch two to four inches thick on the ground around the tree. Begin a couple of inches out from the trunk and extend all the way to the drip line. Lay the mulch down just after the fruit sets or just before the time when you usually start seeing the insects.

As an added precaution against fruit flies, hang yellow sticky traps in trees to catch any that escape the mulch. For green fig beetles, hang cans filled halfway with a solution of 50 percent sugar and 50 percent water on tree limbs. The beetles are attracted to the solution and fall into the water and drown.

PHEROMONE TRAPS
Pheromones are substances produced by one organism that influence the behavior or physiology of another organism of the same species. A female gypsy moth produces a pheromone that can attract males that are miles away. Most commercially available pheromones are in the form of sex pheromone traps, used to lure insects looking for a mate or as signals to disrupt mating. These synthetic pheromones are now being produced in the laboratory and are quite species-specific. Pheromone traps attract only adult insects, so can reduce the number of adults that lay eggs, hopefully making a good dent in the population.

There are several different types of pheromone traps. In one, a pheromone lure is placed inside a cardboard container lined with very sticky material. The insect flies in for a rendezvous with a would-be mate, only to find itself stuck to the container walls. These traps come in various shapes and sizes. Anyone familiar with gypsy moth or pantry traps will recognize this sticky trap. Another pheromone trap lures the insect with the same promise but then catches it inside a no-exit container. You can catch Japanese beetles with this kind.

Pheromone traps cannot be made at home; you have to purchase them. Follow the manufacturer's instructions carefully, and never touch the pheromone capsule or strip with your bare hands. Traps should be replaced whenever dust or debris reduces the trap's stickiness or in about one month.

Here's a list of a few of the common pests for which pheromone traps are available. More are being developed all the time. Check with nurseries for the traps available in your area, or refer to the buying guide at the back of this book for companies that make pheromone traps.

Apple maggots	Flour moths
Bagworms	Fruit flies
Black cutworms	Gypsy moths
Cabbage loopers	Oblique-banded leaf rollers
Cherry maggots	Oriental fruit moths
Cigarette beetles	Peach tree borers
Codling moths	Red-banded leaf rollers
Corn earworms	Spotted tentiform leafminers
European corn borers	

TRAP CROPS

Planting trap crops is a great way to catch insects that really love a specific plant. (Of course, this solution will not work if that is the crop you want to grow!) When the insects appear on the trap crop plant, dispose of them as follows:

~ Shake the plant to dislodge the insects into a bucket of soapy water. (This works best early in the morning.)

~ Hand-pick the insects off the plant. (This works well with caterpillars.)

~ Cover the plant with a piece of cloth and pull the entire plant up with the insects still on it; dispose.

~ Spray the insects on the trap crop plant with insecticidal soap to kill them.

Plant a few of these trap crops in and around your garden if you have a problem with these insects:

~ Aphids: Plant cabbages. Aphids love them. If you want to grow cabbages, try planting nasturtiums nearby. Nasturtiums will also work next to beans and zucchini.

~ Cabbage loopers: Plant hyssop, a herb, to attract the butterflies that lay the eggs of the caterpillar near cabbage plants.

~ Flea beetles: Plant radishes in spring.

~ Harlequin bugs: Plant turnip greens in late summer. Destroy bugs as you see them on the plant.

~ Mexican bean beetles: Plant bush beans before pole beans to attract the beetles and reduce their numbers before you plant your pole beans.

~ Squash bugs: Plant zucchini before summer squash to catch them and reduce their numbers.

Whatever pest you have, use the plant it loves best in your garden this year to make a trap crop to get rid of it next year. Plant a few of these bait plants along the edges of your garden and some more of them in the center of your garden. The insects may well find the plants along the edges and leave the plants in the center for you!

USING ROW COVERS TO CONTROL INSECT PESTS

Row covers can provide a safe and effective barrier against insect pests. Row covers are made of lightweight textiles that will stand up to the elements for many years. They are usually available in many sizes at local nurseries. Here's how to use row covers effectively against specific insects:

~ Asparagus beetles: Place floating row covers over emerging asparagus spears in the spring when adults first appear. Leave covers on throughout the season. Remove at the end of the season when it's time to remove the old fronds.

~ Blister beetles: Protect plants with floating row covers in mid-summer if beetle adults become a big problem. Larvae feed on grasshopper eggs and are beneficial.

~ Cabbage maggots: Cover seedlings with a floating row cover and bury the edges of the cover in the soil to prevent the flies from laying eggs in the soil. Allow plenty of room in the row cover for the growing plant.

~ Carrot rust flies: Cover seedbeds with a floating row cover and bury the edges of the cover in the soil before the seedlings emerge. Allow plenty of room for the carrot plants to grow, and leave row cover in place until harvest.

~ Carrot weevils: Cover seedbeds with a floating row cover before the seedlings emerge and the beetles lay eggs on the stems of the carrots. Bury the edges to prevent weevils from crawling underneath.

~ Colorado potato beetles: Cover susceptible plants with floating row covers from planting time until midseason. Potato beetles prefer to nibble on young plants.

~ Cucumber beetles (spotted) or corn rootworms: Cover seedlings and plants with floating row covers and bury edges so beetles can't lay eggs in the soil next to plants. Allow plenty of room in row cover for growing plants.

~ Cucumber beetles (striped): Cover seedlings with floating row covers and mulch in between plants with straw to discourage beetles. Plants such as squash may need to be hand-pollinated.

~ Diamondback moths: Cover plants with floating row covers to prevent moths from laying eggs on the leaves of the plant.

~ Flea beetles: Cover plants with floating row covers until adults begin to die off in early July. Row covers also provide shade, which the insects do not like.

~ Imported cabbageworms: Cover growing plants with floating row covers to prevent the butterflies from laying eggs on the plant. Butterflies produce three to five generations each year, and covers may need to stay on throughout the season until harvest. To protect cabbage heads from becoming infested, sink a large tomato cage over the heads. Then cover the cage with netting or row cover material to prevent the cabbage butterflies from laying eggs on the heads.

~ Japanese beetles: Cover plants with floating row covers to prevent adults from feeding on plants in heavy infestations.

~ Leaf miners: Cover seedlings with floating row covers to prevent adult flies from laying eggs on the leaves of the plants.

~ Mexican bean beetles: Cover seedlings of bean plants with floating row covers and keep them covered until they are large enough to withstand the damage of the adult beetles feeding on them.

~ Onion maggots: Cover onion or leek seedlings with floating row covers and bury the edges in the soil to prevent the adult flies from laying eggs at the bases of the plants.

~ Strawberry root weevils: Cover plants with floating row covers and bury edges close to base of the strawberry plants to prevent the adults from feeding on them.

~ Tarnished plant bugs: Cover plants with a floating row cover to prevent adults from laying eggs on plant leaves.

USING HOT WATER TO CONTROL INSECTS

Finally, plain old hot water can be a very effective insect and plant control substance.

TO CONTROL INSECTS IN THE SOIL (ANTS, WASPS, AND SO ON)

Pour a couple of gallons of boiling water directly on the mound of an anthill or anywhere you see insects living in the soil. When dealing with fire ants or wasps, be quick: carefully walk up to the mound, pour quickly, and then back away fast. The insects that are not killed will try to escape the nest. It is best to do this in the late evening when temperatures are still warm and the insects are still near the surface but not active outside the nest. Although the hot water usually doesn't kill all the ants or insects on the first try, you can get rid of them or at least reduce their numbers considerably with repeated dousings.

Are you bothered by slugs? Just a little hot water poured onto a slug will do the trick. Have the water ready when you lift the boards you've put down as slug traps.

You can use boiling water on termites you find in deck boards too! Just be sure keep the water from running onto your lawn or prize plants.

TO CONTROL INSECTS ON PLANTS

Hot water makes an effective quick spray to kill soft-bodied insects like aphids, mites, whiteflies, and mealybugs. The water should be between 120 and 150 degrees. It only takes a second or two of spraying to do the trick.

Connect a hose to your hot water heater or a basement or garage sink for easy spraying. Woody plants tolerate hot water better than some ornamental plants, but always test the hot water on a few leaves to see if it causes any damage before treating a whole plant.

Make-It-Yourself Fertilizers, Mulches, and Compost

Diagnosing a plant nutrient problem can be difficult. How often have you gone to a nursery with a piece of sickly looking plant in hand, hoping for a miracle cure? Let's say you have had your soil tested and were able to rule out any problems there. And you try to grow plants that are well suited to both your soil and your climate conditions. If you still have problems, use the chart on the following pages to help you become your own plant doctor, then mix up the remedy.

USING ORGANIC FERTILIZERS

Organic fertilizers provide plants with all the nutrients and trace elements they need in a balanced formula, and most importantly, they provide organic matter to the soil. They are naturally slow-release fertilizers, providing the nutrients to the plants when the plants need them, unlike synthetic fertilizers that hit a plant all at once and force it into a flush of growth.

UNDERSTANDING THE NUMBERS Every fertilizer contains trace elements, which plants need in minute quantities, and major nutrients, which are needed in larger amounts. The formula of the three major nutrients— nitrogen (N), phosphorous (P), and potassium (K)—is shown on labels in the percentage by weight in which they are contained, as in the chart on the next page.

Nutrient	Symptoms of Deficiency	Sources of Nutrient	Average of N-P-K values
Nitrogen Needed for all stages of plant growth.	Leaves are yellow and plant is light green in color; plant often stunted.	Alfalfa meal	(3-1-2)
		Bat guano	(10-3-1)
		Blood meal	(12-1-1)
		Compost	(1-1-1)
		Cottonseed meal	(7-2-2)
		Earthworm castings	(1.5-2-1)
		Fish emulsion	(5-2-2)
		Manure, chicken or turkey	(6-4-2)
		Manure, cow, dried	(2-1-1)
		Manure, horse, dried	(4-1-1)
		Manure, rabbit	(3-2-1)
		Sewer sludge compost	(5-3-0)
		Soybean meal	(6-0-0)
Phosphorus Increases the rate of plant maturity and strengthens plant stems.	Leaves appear red, purple, or very dark green, and growth may be stunted. Weak flower or fruit production.	Bone meal	(2-12-0)
		Colloidal phosphate	(0-18-0)
		Fish meal	(7-13-31)
		Rock phosphate	(0-31-0)
Potassium Required for the formation of sugars, starches, and proteins in a plant.	Leaf tips and edges are yellow, often turning brown. Stems are generally weak. Increased susceptibility to disease.	Granite sand	(0-0-5)
		Greensand	(0-2-5)
		Kelp extract	(2-1-[4 to 13])
		Kelp meal	(1-0-8)
		Sul-Po-Mag	(0-0-22)
		Wood ashes	(0-trace-[5 to 10])
Magnesium Supports necessary enzyme activity.	Older or lower leaves are yellow, but veins are still green. Plant may be stunted.	Dolomitic lime	
		Epsom salts	
		Fish emulsion	
Zinc Important for sweet taste in fruits and vegetables.	Leaves are yellow and thickened, but veins are still green. Poor bud formation and small terminal leaves.	Chelated zinc spray	
		Kelp extract	
		Kelp meal	
		Zinc sulfate	

Nutrient	Symptoms of Deficiency	Sources of Nutrient
Calcium Needed for water uptake, cell development and division.	Buds and young leaves die back at tips. Increased susceptibility to disease.	Calcium carbonate Gypsum Oyster and clam shells Rock phosphate Wood ashes
Iron Important for nitrogen fixation and photosynthesis. Also green color in plants.	Young leaves are yellow but veins are still green. Growth may be stunted.	Chelated iron spray Chicken manure, dried Compost Greensand Kelp meal and extract Wood ashes
Boron Affects cell development, flowering, fruiting, and other functions.	Plant appears bushy. Growing tips and new buds die and lower branches send out new shoots.	Boric acid solution Compost Granite dust Kelp extract Rock phosphate
Sulfur Increases protein content and promotes seed production.	Young leaves appear light green overall or yellow; growth is usually stunted.	Blackstrap or horticultural molasses Compost Elemental sulfur Gypsum
Copper Important nutrient for disease resistance.	Young leaves pale with brown tips, often wilted.	Copper sulfate Kelp meal and extract
Manganese Important for photosynthesis; aids in phosphate metabolism.	Dead spots, while tissue between veins on young leaves.	Epsom salts Kelp meal and extract Sul-Po-Mag
Molybdenum Needed for nitrogen fixation; unavailable in acid soils.	Young or upper leaves are yellow but veins are still green. Growth often stunted.	Kelp extract Kelp meal

HOW ORGANIC FERTILIZERS WORK

Following are some organic fertilizers and a brief description of what they do for plants and soil.

~ Alfalfa meal provides nutrient benefits for both plants and soil organisms. It contains a plant-growth regulator called *triacontanol* as well as folic acid, trace minerals, and many vitamins. It supplies sugars, starches, proteins, and sixteen amino acids.

~ Bat guano, as the name implies, is the feces of bats. It is a good all-purpose fertilizer that provides nitrogen, phosphorous, and trace elements. Many gardeners use it as a supplemental fertilizer for their flowers once or twice a year during the growing season. Bat guano has also been shown to have natural fungicidal qualities.

~ Biostimulators, also called biostimulants, are usually bought in liquid form. The liquid contains various minerals, enzymes, vitamins, and sometimes microbes to stimulate microbial activity in the soil.

~ Blood meal, made from blood produced in slaughterhouses, is often used to repel rabbits. It is a good source of nitrogen and phosphorus and is often mixed with cottonseed meal to provide an all-purpose fertilizer. Although expensive, it is probably worth it if you have a rabbit problem.

~ Bone meal is a good source of phosphorous and calcium, which makes up between 2 percent and 5 percent of the total composition. Bone meal is often used with heavy feeders such as tomatoes and bulbs.

~ Boric acid solution is made by combining boric acid crystals with water (usually two teaspoons of boric acid to one gallon of water). It is commonly used to treat fruit trees with boron deficiency.

~ Calcium carbonate, or calcite limestone, is a good source of calcium.

~ Chelated is a term referring to organic compounds that have inorganic metal molecules, such as copper, iron, manganese, and zinc, attached. This arrangement allows the metal molecules to be available to plants. Chelated nutrients are used when a nutrient is needed quickly to correct a specific deficiency in a plant.

~ Chicken manure is a fertilizer high in nitrogen that is obtained from commercial chicken farms. It is best to compost this material before using.

~ Colloidal phosphate is an excellent source of phosphorus, calcium, and trace minerals. This mixture of phosphate particles in a clay base is usually quite economical. Mined in Florida, the phosphate particles will not dissolve in water, which makes the stuff long-lasting.

~ Compost is the best organic fertilizer there is. Before chemical fertilizers were invented, compost was the only real fertilizer. Compost is high in humus, humic acid, and soil microorganisms. The chemical analysis varies depending on the ingredients the compost was made with. Compost can be used on all plants.

~ Copper sulfate is a copper and sulfur compound used to control various fungal and bacterial diseases. It is also used when a copper deficiency is detected in a plant.

~ Cottonseed meal is a good organic source of nitrogen and trace elements. It has an acidic pH and is often an ingredient in all-purpose fertilizers.

~ Cow manure is a readily available and inexpensive fertilizer. It is usually recommended that it be composted before using, but many gardeners have success with fresh manure. This is a preferred food source for earthworms and soil organisms. As with all good things, a little cow manure goes a long way. It should not be overused.

~ Dolomitic lime is a form of ground limestone used commonly to increase the pH level of alkaline soil. It is also a source of magnesium and calcium.

~ Earthworm castings are an excellent all-purpose fertilizer that not only supplies nutrients but also microorganisms, over sixty trace minerals, and humus. Castings will not burn plants and have been found to be stable in the ground for five years, making them an excellent time-release fertilizer. For heavy calcium feeders like tomatoes, extra calcium should be added for best results.

~ Epsom salts, or magnesium sulfate, is used to treat soils and plants deficient in magnesium and sulfur. Because of its high salt content, it should not be used on soils that are already high in salt.

~ Fish emulsion is a concentrated liquid form of fertilizer made from fish. High in nitrogen, it is used as a soil fertilizer and as a foliar fertilizer. One drawback is the odor, which lasts about a day after application.

~ Fish meal is a natural fertilizer made in meal form that is high in nitrogen and phosphorus.

~ Granite sand, the residue from granite quarries, is a good source of potash and trace minerals.

~ Greensand is *glauconite*, an undersea deposit of iron-potassium silicate. It's a good source of potash and is generally used with other fertilizers.

~ Gypsum is calcium sulfate, a good source of calcium and sulfur. It is an inexpensive material to use for neutralizing acidic soils, and it also helps to break up heavy clay soils so air and water can penetrate.

~ Horse manure is a very inexpensive fertilizer—if you happen to have a stable nearby. It is higher in nitrogen than cow manure so care should be taken with it if used around plants. However, it's great in the compost pile.

~ Humate is a good source of humic acid, carbon, and trace minerals. It is a low-grade coal that can be found in liquid and dry forms.

~ Kelp extract is a liquid form of seaweed that is a great source of trace minerals and plant hormones. It also acts as a chelating substance that makes nutrients in fertilizers more available to the plants. It is often mixed with fish emulsion to provide an all-purpose fertilizer.

~ Kelp meal is made from seaweed and has lots of trace minerals. It stimulates root growth and is a source of plant hormones. It's a great agent for improving the soil's structure.

~ Lava dust is very small particles from lava gravel. It is used primarily as a soil amendment.

~ Lime is a major source of calcium and magnesium. Dolomitic lime is used commonly to adjust the pH of alkaline soils.

~ Molasses is a good source of sulfur, potash, and other trace minerals and is also a stimulant and food for microorganisms in the soil.

~ Oyster and clam shells in ground form are a good source of calcium.

~ Rabbit manure is a good manure fertilizer. It can be used fresh or composted first.

·· Rock phosphate is a by-product of phosphate mining and a good source of slow-release phosphorus.

~ Root stimulator is a term used to refer to a material that stimulates microorganisms and root growth.

~ Sewer sludge compost is the solid material from a sewer treatment facility that has been composted. Often used as a lawn fertilizer, it shouldn't be used as a vegetable garden fertilizer.

~ Soybean meal is made from soybeans and is used primarily as a source of nitrogen or as a soil amendment.

~ Sul-Po-Mag is a naturally mined mineral that is a good source of sulfur, potassium, and magnesium.

·· Turkey manure, like chicken manure, is high in nitrogen and often used in compost.

~ Wood ashes are a good, quickly soluble source of phosphorus. However, they are alkaline and should be used cautiously if your soil has a high pH level.

ACID-LOVING PLANT HELP

Why is it that we love plants that grow in soil other than what we have? Many of our favorite garden plants love acid soils with a pH below 6.5, such as azaleas, butterfly weed, camellias, cardinal flowers, ferns, gardenias, oaks, and spruces. Unfortunately, many soils west of the Mississippi are quite alkaline. What to do?

First, check to see exactly what the pH of your soil is. Test kits are available at most garden shops and nurseries. Follow the directions carefully and test several areas of your yard. You maybe surprised to find that they differ. If you have alkaline soil, try one of these methods to increase your soil's acidity.

One solution is to add vinegar—yes, ordinary distilled vinegar. The acidity of the vinegar is just what the soil needs to lower its pH. Just mix 2 cups vinegar with 2 gallons water. Pour the solution on the ground around the drip line of the plant. Repeat every three months during the growing season.

Another solution is to add coffee grounds. This old advice is still good. Work leftover coffee grounds directly around the bases of acid-loving plants. Some say to dry the grounds before working them in, but this is not essential. Or, add the grounds to your compost pile and then use the finished compost with the grounds in it around your plants.

Oak leaves also have a lot of acid in them. Make an acid tea. Fill a large bucket halfway with oak leaves. Add water to fill the bucket. Let stand until the water looks like nice strong tea, then remove the leaves. Water plants with the solution. Add the leftover leaves to your compost pile.

Add compost to the soil around the plant, and the plant will do the rest. A University of Connecticut study found that adding an inch of compost around acid-loving plants once a year made the soil slightly acidic and ideal for the plants.

BLOOMING HOUSEPLANT FERTILIZER

Flowering houseplants need a good nutrient boost to put on a really great show. However, if you fertilize your plants but they still look pale and sickly, the problem might be the water you are using.

When the soil is either too acidic or too alkaline some nutrients become unavailable to the plant. Also, many of us live in areas with hard water, which tends to be alkaline. Bringing the water back to a neutral pH of 7 will also help a houseplant's soil to shift toward neutral, making nutrients more available to the plant. A simple test with litmus paper can tell you if your water is acidic, alkaline, or neutral.

To correct slightly alkaline or hard water, try this simple method: Mix a tablespoon of vinegar (either cider or white) with a gallon of water. You may wish to check the pH of the solution with litmus paper to see if it's neutral, then correct proportions if necessary. Use this solution to water your houseplants.

It is easy to make a good all-purpose organic houseplant fertilizer. One of the best is fish emulsion, which is full of nitrogen, is inexpensive, and works well. Simply follow bottle directions and you'll have beautiful green foliage. To supplement the fish emulsion and give your houseplants an extra boost of potassium and phosphorus for flowering, try this recipe:

Fish emulsion supplement

> *1 part cottonseed or alfalfa meal*
> *1 part bonemeal*
> *1 part wood ashes*
>   *(or kelp meal if you don't want to use alkaline wood ashes)*

Mix together and apply at a rate of 1 teaspoon per 6-inch pot every sixty days until the plant finishes flowering for the season. Sprinkle around base of potted plant and work in gently.

BULB FERTILIZER

Those of you who grow beautiful flowers from bulbs know that they often fade out because of lack of nutrients. So make a great bulb fertilizer to keep those bulbs flowering.

4 to 5 pounds bonemeal
(added before planting)
1 part cottonseed meal
1 part bonemeal
1 part greensand

Start by working the 4 to 5 pounds of bonemeal into the top layer of your bed. This amount will cover about 100 square feet. Then mix last three ingredients together. Be sure to wear a dust mask to avoid breathing in dust particles. Plant bulbs in the bed, sprinkling the fertilizer on top as soon as leaves begin to emerge. Apply about 2 pounds of fertilizer for every 100 square feet. Try to keep the fertilizer off the foliage. Water lightly to dissolve fertilizer slowly into the soil. When flowers begin to fade, apply a ¼-inch layer of compost.

You can substitute a good organic fertilizer with a N-P-K value of 5-10-10 instead of making your own, but apply it twice: 1 pound when the leaves emerge and 1 pound again when flowers fade. If you decide to use a time-release fertilizer, however, apply it only once.

CAMELLIA AND AZALEA FOOD

Here's a recipe for a wonderful organic fertilizer your acid-loving plants like camellias and azaleas will love.

2 parts cottonseed meal
1 part kelp meal
1 part fish meal

Mix together. Use 1 pound of fertilizer per inch of trunk diameter. Start feeding plants in March, then every sixty days through growing season.

CITRUS FERTILIZER AND SWEETENER

Nothing is as wonderful as a sweet and juicy orange, lime, or lemon. To make your trees produce tasty citrus, try this recipe.

> *1 part fish meal*
> *1 part hoof and horn meal*
> *1 part kelp meal*
> *1 part cottonseed meal*
> *1 cup either Citrus Grower's Mix, Vim, or Sarvon*
>   *(commercial organic sources of micronutrients)*

Mix all ingredients together and apply 2 pounds per inch of trunk diameter. Cover with compost. Apply twice a year.

GENERAL-PURPOSE ORGANIC FERTILIZER

Here is a great all-purpose fertilizer for many types of perennial plants and bushes.

> *1 part alfalfa meal*
> *1 part fish meal*
> *1 part greensand*
> *1 part gypsum*
> *½ part bonemeal*

Mix all ingredients and spread 1 cup around each plant or bush. For very large bushes use up to 2 cups. Mix the fertilizer into the first few inches of the soil with a hoe or cultivator. Fertilize once in early spring and again in early summer.

GREEN MANURE FERTILIZER

Green manure is a term used for grasses and legumes grown and then tilled under. It is cheap and easy to use, and in most cases it is faster-acting than compost. In severe-winter areas, a hearty green manure crop can protect the soil and give the added benefit of nutrients and organic material to the soil in spring.

Plants to fertilize other plants

To use plants to add nutrients to the soil, first choose annual grasses and legumes that are good at nitrogen fixation—taking nitrogen from the air and converting it into a form that plants can use. Legumes are great at this, and some gardeners only use legumes as their crop's nitrogen source. However, if you grow grasses and grains as well, when you till them under you not only add extra nitrogen to the soil but great organic matter as well. A good mix of legumes to grasses and grains is this: 60 percent legumes, 30 percent grasses, and 10 percent grains.

Peas and beans are the most common legumes to use for green manure. Hairy vetch, buckwheat, rye, and oats are the most common grasses and grains. Many seed companies will mix a blend of seeds to your specific needs. Check the buying guide at the back of this book for green manure seed companies, or ask your favorite seed company for its recommendations for green manure crops in your area.

Plant green manure crops in spring, summer, or fall—or whenever you have time between crops. Prepare the soil as you would for a vegetable garden: Loosen it and then smooth it down for a nice seedbed. Now broadcast the green manure seeds at about 2 to 3 pounds of seed per 1,000 square feet of seedbed area. Some seed companies recommend as much as 5 pounds of seeds per 1,000 square feet, so check the recommended application rates for the blends of seeds you buy. When only planting grasses or grains, 2 pounds per 1,000 feet is usually enough. Cover the seeds with a light topping of soil or compost and water.

Allow the plants to grow until just before they bloom, then till them under. Wait two to four weeks to allow the plants to break down in the soil and release their nitrogen. Then you are ready to plant your desired crops.

IRON FERTILIZERS

Lots of plants—hydrangeas, for example—can use a good shot of iron once in a while to stay healthy or cure a mild case of iron deficiency. You know the signs: the leaves are yellow with still-green veins.

You can recycle used scouring pads to make a simple and easy-to-use iron fertilizer. Place 1 used steel wool pad in a container with 1 quart water. Let it set for a week, then discard pad. The next time you water your plants, mix 1 to 2 tablespoons of the solution to every gallon of water.

For a quick-acting source of iron, make a foliar or leaf spray from seaweed or kelp extract. Use 1 tablespoon kelp extract per each gallon of water or as directed on the bottle and spray biweekly.

For long-term slow release of iron, try sprinkling dried chicken manure, compost, greensand, or wood ashes around each plant once in the fall.

A note of caution: do not use wood ashes on alkaline soils. As with other nutrients, a high-alkaline soil can make iron unavailable to plants. Often just lowering the pH of the soil to 6.0 to 6.8 will eliminate the iron problem. To do this, try working peat moss, manure, or other acid-building organic material into alkaline soils.

LEAF OR FOLIAR FERTILIZERS

Although many people overlook it, a good way of fertilizing plants is through the leaves. It has been estimated that only 10 percent of nutrients are absorbed by the plant with pour-on soil fertilizers. In contrast, a good 90 percent of the nutrients are absorbed when the fertilizer is applied directly to the plant's leaves.

Here are some tips for applying a leaf or foliar fertilizer:

~ Apply the fertilizer in a fine mist and spray all leaf surfaces.

~ Apply in the early morning or late evening to prevent burning and when the plant's pores (or stomata) are open.

~ For best results, apply to plants that are actively growing, are about to bloom, or have just set fruit.

Kelp extract spray

Spray diluted liquid seaweed (kelp extract) or mix seaweed powder into a solution for added zinc, iron, copper, manganese, or molybdenum. Seaweed powder is generally much less expensive than kelp extract, yet will give the same results. Mix 1 tablespoon liquid seaweed or seaweed powder with 1 gallon of water. Apply weekly until plants set fruit or blooming begins.

For plants that need extra nitrogen with their minerals, combine fish emulsion with the seaweed or kelp extract. Here's the recipe:

*1½ tablespoons liquid seaweed
    or kelp extract
1½ tablespoons of fish emulsion
1 gallon water*

Mix ingredients together. Place solution in a sprayer or mist bottle and spray seedlings every two weeks, or as needed for older plants.

Compost and worm tea sprays

Compost too can make a nutrient-rich leaf spray. To make compost tea, fill a waterproof can ⅛ to ¼ full of compost, then add enough water to fill the can. Let steep overnight or until solution looks like weak iced tea. Strain and place liquid in a spray bottle and spray weekly on fast-growing plants, monthly on slow-growing plants. Do not use manure compost to make a tea that will be used on vegetables or fruit because there's a slight chance the manure will carry *E. coli* bacteria.

Worm castings also make good nutrient- and trace mineral–rich tea. Prepare the tea as you would compost tea but only fill the can ⅛ of the way with the castings. Castings are water soluble and will dissolve fairly quickly. Spray fast-growing plants weekly and slow-growing or house-plants monthly.

ROSE FERTILIZERS

Use this organic rose food recipe to keep your blooms and bushes beautiful.

1 part hoof and horn meal

1 part chicken manure

1 part cottonseed meal

2 parts bonemeal

1 part kelp meal

Mix ingredients together. Apply 1 cup per plant every sixty days.

To perk up your roses during the midseason, try this suggestion that appeared in *American Rose* magazine: Mix 1 to 2 tablespoons powdered brewer's yeast with 1 gallon of water. Use solution to water your rose bushes. Foliage will be greener, growth sturdier, and blooms better.

WORM CASTING FERTILIZER AND TONIC

Earthworm castings make an excellent fertilizer and tonic for plants. One study found that replacing the basic plant compost mixed into garden soil with vermicompost—a mixture of worm castings and bacterially composted bedding and food—resulted in a 36 percent greater crop yield the first year of planting. The plants not only grew better but were healthier and more disease-resistant. Earthworm castings have even been used to treat sick plants with good results.

There are several ways to incorporate worm castings or vermicompost into your garden or houseplants.

~ Work the castings directly into the soil. Just sprinkle on, rake in, and forget. Castings will not burn your plants, and according to one study, the level of nutrients in the soil after the addition of the castings was stable for over five years. Apply about a ¼-inch thickness of castings to garden beds or lawns.

~ Use as a mulch. Spread castings about 2 inches thick inside the drip line of a tree or plant, being sure to stay away from the trunk. Use in an area that remains a bit moist, because dry castings can form a hard crust that repels water.

~ Add to transplants. When setting out small garden seedlings or transplanting mature plants, place some castings directly in the hole that the plant will go in.

~ Make worm tea. If you have a worm bin, collect the drainage water. This water has diluted worm castings in it. Mix it with an equal part of water for houseplants or use it undiluted in the garden. You can also make your own worm tea by diluting purchased worm castings in water. Use about ¼ cup of worm castings per gallon of water for general feeding. Make the solution stronger for a soil drench for stressed plants. Worm tea makes an excellent foliar fertilizer, too. (See leaf or foliar recipes on page 87.)

TREE FERTILIZERS

Every gardening magazine has another fertilizer that it proclaims to be perfect for trees, whether they are fruit or ornamental trees. But before you can fertilize your trees you must know where to put the fertilizer. Here are some general tips on feeding trees.

~ To fertilize young trees, place the fertilizer from 1 inch inside the tree's drip line to 3 inches outside of it to reach most of the tree's feeder roots. The drip line is where the tree's limbs extend to, and most feeder roots will be in the top 12 to 18 inches of the soil.

~ To fertilize mature trees, first find the root zone by measuring the trunk's diameter 1 foot above the ground. If the trunk measures 12 inches, then the feeder roots will extend out about 12 feet (because 1 inch is equivalent to 1 foot). Most feeder roots form a band around the outer two-thirds of this number. If the outer number is 12 feet, multiply that by two-thirds to get the inner band number. So in this case, the feeder roots extend from 8 to 12 feet away from the tree's trunk.

Young tree fertilizer

If you amend the soil with bonemeal and organic material when you plant a new tree, keeping the young tree fertilized can be quite easy. Wait to fertilize until the tree becomes established—usually three to four weeks. Then apply a good ¼-inch layer of compost over the root zone at least once a year. Apply a good organic fertilizer two or three times a year. Mix a solution of fish emulsion at a rate of 1 teaspoon to 5 gallons of water. Pour on root zone three times a year. Increase teaspoons of fish emulsion by 1 teaspoon for each year of age. (For example, a five-year-old tree would get 5 teaspoons of emulsion to 5 gallons of water.)

Mature tree fertilizer

Most mature trees in good health need little fertilizing because the fallen leaves give their nutrients back. However, the trees that live in our lawns often need a little extra help because we rake up the leaves, and if there is grass growing under the tree, we mow it and cart it away. Instead, use a mulching lawn mower if you have grass growing under a tree. The grass clippings will break down and supply extra nitrogen to the tree and the grass. Also, apply a ¼-inch layer of compost around the root zone once a year. If you think your trees need a bit more fertilizing, make this recipe and top-dress it with compost once a year:

1 part cottonseed meal

1 part rock phosphate

1 part greensand

1 part gypsum

Mix all ingredients together, being sure to wear a dust mask while you do it. Apply 1 pound of fertilizer for every inch of trunk diameter to root zone. Apply compost on top.

USING SEED-FREE MANURE

Many gardeners love what cow manure can do for their gardens but not the weeds it brings in. Manure from other farm animals contains fewer weed seeds but still has some. What can you do?

Build a hot compost pile

This is sometimes easier said than done for the novice composter. The temperature of the pile must rise to at least 140 degrees to kill weed seeds. (See "Tips on Making Compost" on page 93 for more helpful suggestions about making compost.)

Block out the weeds

Spread that manure, but before you're done add another layer of light-blocking mulch. Anything that blocks out sunlight will do, from bark to newspaper. Usually, 3 inches of loose mulch or 10 sheets of newspaper are sufficient. Black plastic will block the sunlight and quickly age the manure at the same time. Now you have the fertilizing benefits of manure without germinating more weeds.

FREE FERTILIZERS

Finding a good organic fertilizer is good, but finding a free one is better. Here are a few:

~ Eggshells. Eggshells can be made into a calcium-rich tonic. Tomatoes and other plants feed heavily on calcium, especially when blooming. Just save the eggshells from cooking until you have about ¼ cup. Add the eggshells to a gallon of water and let sit a few days to a week. Then use the water to water your plants. Keep a bottle steeping while you collect more eggshells. For a more diluted calcium tonic, just use the water in which you boiled some eggs.

~ Fish water food. If you are lucky enough to have an aquarium or just a fish bowl, don't throw away the old water. Use it to water your houseplants. This can really help you cut down on purchases of commercial fish emulsion.

~ Free composting materials. A local mushroom farm, restaurant, grocery store, landscaper, or arborist may love to get rid of some green waste that would be perfect for your compost pile.

~ Free compost. Many landfills now compost their green waste and then give it away. You need only bring your truck or a garbage can and take it away.

~ Manure. Manure tea is a great fertilizer for seedlings or mature plants. If you're lucky enough to have a friend with a horse, he or she would probably be happy to provide you with a manure supply. If not, check with local stables, dairies, fairgrounds, or zoos to see if manure is available at little or no cost. Bagged manure is good too, if free sources are not available. An added benefit is that earthworms love the stuff! To make manure tea:

1 shovelful horse, cow, or
    poultry manure (fresh or aged)
1 large piece of cloth
5-gallon bucket

Put manure in piece of cloth and tie it closed. Place package into a bucket and fill bucket with water. Let steep for 2 to 3 days. Remove manure bag and discard in compost pile. Dilute solution if necessary until it looks like weak iced tea. Now use as a soil drench or a foliar fertilizer. Expand ingredients proportionately to fill a trash can for lots of manure tea.

MAKING YOUR OWN MULCH

Mulches help conserve water, reduce insects, reduce soil compaction, and prevent weeds and soil erosion. Mulching is also a great way to recycle yard wastes into useful material that feeds the soil and plants. In areas with very cold winters, mulches stabilize the soil temperature. This helps to protect the microorganisms that suffer from rapid temperature fluctuations. Winter mulches also help protect roots of perennials and permanent crops from cold damage.

MULCH 101

Spread mulch thickly or thinly, depending on the plants and the type of mulch. For woody plants, a three-inch layer is usual. Start the mulch two to three inches away from the trunk to keep mice from chewing on the bark and prevent rot. For shallow-rooted plants, like azaleas, put on a thin layer.

The soil under a thick layer of mulch in the summer will be around 85 degrees, whereas bare ground will be around 120 degrees.

    Use a mulch that breaks down in one season for your annuals and perennials. Leaf, straw, and grass mulches are great for this purpose. You can dig up and turn the soil without worrying about mulch that is not broken down at the end of the growing season. Grass clippings that are not composted first shouldn't be put on too thickly—about one inch is right. Do this regularly throughout the season to keep the grass from matting down and preventing water from soaking in properly. Mulches that compact easily, like grass and leaves, may need to be fluffed up periodically.

For woody plants and shrubs, use mulches that break down slowly. These mulches don't have to replaced each season and provide long-term protection. Bark, chipped wood, and hull mulches are great here.

Pine needles make a good mulch for acid-loving plants. The needles break down and add a lower pH to the soil, which is preferred by plants such as azaleas and rhododendrons.

Many gardeners like to use partially decomposed compost about three to five inches thick on garden beds. It breaks down slowly, adding nutrients over a long period. Be careful if using fresh manure as a mulch because it can burn plants and also carries weed seeds.

Sawdust or finely ground woody plants can also be used, but put them on the surface only. If mixed into the soil, these materials can tie up nitrogen and steal it from plants. Small-particle mulches also tend to mat down and need to be fluffed up a bit periodically.

To keep paths weed-free longer, place newspaper or cardboard down, then add a thick layer of mulch. Mulches that break down slowly, like bark and wood chips, make a good path.

Some mulches repel animals and insects. Eucalyptus mulch is a great natural insect repellent. Cocoa mulch, made from the hulls of cocoa beans, smells like chocolate. Cats and snails hate it. Gardeners who use cocoa mulch report that cats won't dig in it and snails and slugs won't cross it.

Probably the worst choice is peat moss. Although it is acid and will lower a soil's pH, be careful with it if you live in a dry area. If it is not kept moist, peat moss can form a dry crust that actually repels water instead of absorbing it. In addition, it is expensive and tends to blow away.

MAKING MULCH

Would you like to have all the mulch you need for your garden, ready and waiting at spring planting time? Better than that, how about it costing you nothing? Sound good? All it takes is a little planning in the fall.

A nice autumn day when dry leaves are falling off the tree like rain is the perfect time to make mulch. Now get a rake, a trash can, plastic trash bags, string trimmer and you are ready.

First, rake up clean leaves and fill a trash can up about halfway. Make sure the leaves are dry! Next, push the string trimmer head down under the leaves in the can. Turn it on, working it in short pulses until the leaves are reduced. Continue chopping until you reach the consistency you want. Place this leaf mulch in plastic bags and close, and store until spring. This is also good way to get more leaves into your recycling bin (if you are not composting them).

A good chipper or shredder also makes quick mulch. Use pruned limbs that are too large for the compost bin.

Here's an easy tip for applying mulch to a newly planted bed. Cover your new plants with old nursery pots. Pick the size that will just cover the plants. Then spread or sprinkle mulch over the planted area. You won't have to worry about the mulch getting onto the new plants or about accidentally stepping on them. When finished, remove the pots.

TIPS ON MAKING COMPOST

Composting is a great idea for many reasons. Most important, it recycles plant nutrients back into the soil. Why buy lots of fertilizers when you have the raw ingredients to make your own?

Many books have been written about the correct way to make compost. Actually, a pile of leaves moved to the side of the yard will eventually decompose all by itself, although it will take some twelve to eighteen months. However, knowing a few basics will really get you started.

What to put in your compost pile

Eggshells	Plant prunings and trimmings
Farm manure except pig	Shells from crabs, lobsters, and so on
Grass clippings	Sod
Hay	Straw
Kitchen vegetable scraps	Used matches
Leaves	Water in which you boiled vegetables
Leftover coffee	Wine corks
Old flower arrangements	

What not to put in your compost pile

Animal products	Cat, dog, or primate manure
Diseased plants	Plants treated with herbicides
Oils	

Perennial weeds like bindweed, or any other hard-to-kill weeds (or make a separate pile for them)

DO YOU NEED A COMPOST BIN?

You don't have to put your compost materials in a bin. Many gardeners still just compost in large piles or windrows in an out-of-the-way corner of their yard. Other people don't like the looks of decaying materials.

You can make a bin from new or recycled materials. Chicken wire, wood, and plastic can all be made into a successful compost bin. In order for the material to decompose efficiently, oxygen needs to enter the pile. The microorganisms that really get a compost pile going require oxygen, so be sure to leave open slats on the sides of your bin for plenty of ventilation.

Trash cans may be made into small compost bins that can be kept anywhere. Make sure the can has a tight-fitting lid, and poke holes for air around the lower half of the can. Add materials to be composted and cover tightly. Roll the can around or shake it to bring more oxygen to the center. When it's ready, use the finished compost right out of the can.

If you don't want to bother with building a pile or making a bin, try hole composting. Dig a six-inch hole with a post hole digger or trowel, throw your kitchen or garden scraps into it, and cover it with dirt. It will soon be compost. You can dig holes in spaces between garden plants or anywhere that compost is needed.

If you decide not to build your own bin and think a pile or a hole is just too messy, you can purchase a bin in a size that will fit your needs. In some areas communal composting bins are available, managed by city parks, gardening clubs, or landfills. If one is available in your area, you can get finished compost there at little or no cost.

STARTING A COMPOST PILE

To start building your compost pile, alternate layers of high-carbon material like dead leaves, straw, and wood chips (browns) with layers of high-nitrogen material like grass clippings, manure, and kitchen scraps (greens). Most compost piles are built with a 50-50 ratio of browns to greens. As you layer the pile, mix the layers with a pitchfork. The last layer should be made of browns, aged compost, or soil.

Moisten each layer as you go. The moisture equivalent of a wrung-out sponge is just about perfect. If a pile is too dry, it slows decomposition and prevents the pile from heating up. With open compost piles or bins in dry areas, you may need to water the bin every day. In contrast, if a pile is too wet, it drives out air and prevents decomposition. It also washes away many nutrients. In wet areas, you may need to put a layer of plastic, dried grass, or straw on top to prevent it from getting waterlogged.

If the pile does get too wet, add newspaper, straw, or sawdust to absorb water.

Turn composting materials every week or two to provide oxygen. The more air that gets to the center of the pile, the faster it will decompose. An average pile turns into finished compost in three to six months. If getting compost as fast as possible is your goal, then turning the pile every one to three days will help. Shovel the outside of the pile into the middle for even composting. Or drill holes in a large-diameter (three- to four-inch) PVC pipe, or some leftover landscape irrigation pipe, and push it into the center of the pile so more air can get in. With this method, you won't have to turn the pile as frequently—and sometimes not at all. Piles may also be built on wire platforms that raise them off the ground, allowing air to enter from the bottom.

Shredded or chopped materials compost faster than larger pieces. Very large pieces of wood can be burned and the ashes added to the pile. When adding material to a bin, never put in a large quantity of any one item at one time. When adding kitchen scraps, always place them in the center of the pile to avoid attracting rodents.

When composting manure, a good mixture is 80 percent plant material to 20 percent manure. A pile that is 100 percent manure will compost too, but your plants will find the finished compost from an 80-20 mixture much nicer.

Finally, don't believe quick composting claims. Depending on weather conditions, the type of pile, and the ingredients, turning raw materials into rich compost can take time. The most important thing is to be patient!

WHAT SIZE IS THE AVERAGE PILE?

The average pile measures four or five feet around the bottom and is as high as four feet. This size is adequate for heating. Piles smaller than three square feet may not get hot enough to kill weed seeds—they need to reach 140 degrees to do so. A good thermometer can help you determine if the pile is getting hot enough.

PROBLEMS IN THE PILE?

If your pile smells sour, then more oxygen needs to get into it. The sour smell is coming from anaerobic bacteria, which live without oxygen. Add some dry carbon material, like dried leaves or twigs, and turn the pile to incorporate more oxygen.

If the pile is not heating up, it is probably too dry. Add more water and turn the pile to ensure that oxygen is getting in. Or the leaves may have matted down into dense layers that do not allow oxygen in. If this is the case, turn the pile and break up these mats.

Uneven heating happens when the edges of the pile are too cool. Try turning the pile more often.

WHEN IS THE COMPOST FINISHED?

The compost is ready when the original ingredients are no longer identifiable. It will smell like a forest floor—a fine, earthy smell. It will be dark brown in color and have a soft and crumbly texture. This usually occurs after the pile has remained at 120 to 150 degrees or more for four days to a week and then cooled down to 100 degrees.

If large pieces remain in your compost when it is finished, you can screen them out and place them in your next compost pile to finish decomposing.

WHAT IS AGED COMPOST?

Aged compost has been allowed to sit for two to four weeks or longer before using to allow the remaining weed seeds to germinate. The weed sprouts are then turned back into the pile. You can turn your pile and then wait as many times as you need in order to rid the compost of weed seeds.

HOW TO USE COMPOST

~ Before planting, mix a 4- to 8-inch layer of compost into a new garden bed.

~ In annual flower beds, add a 1- to 3-inch layer of compost each year.

~ Use it as a mulch in layers of 1 to 6 inches.

~ Use it to fertilize lawns. Spread ¼ to ½ inch of compost on your lawn every year.

~ Sprinkle it as a topdressing on houseplants.

~ Use it to make potting soil.

WHAT'S THAT IN MY COMPOST BIN?

Many organisms besides those that actually do the decomposition like to live in a compost pile. Be ready to see crawling creatures.

This list gives a few examples of the creatures you are likely to find and some control methods if you feel they are necessary. Remember, most controls are not necessary, and some are even toxic to the earthworms and microorganisms you need for decomposition.

Ants

Ants are everywhere and probably in your compost pile, too. They are always on the search for food, and in your compost pile they have found something tasty. There isn't much you can do to control ants in compost piles on the ground, but with a compost pile in a bin try the barrier approach. There are many substances that ants will not cross, and you can use one to block them from entering:

Cayenne pepper	Mentholated rub
Cleanser	Talcum powder
Eucalyptus oil	Tanglefoot or any sticky substance
Lemon juice	Water
Lemon-scented oil	

Depending on where your compost bin is located, you can decide which one will best suit your needs. Unfortunately, none works forever and each must be reapplied periodically.

Centipedes

Centipedes are fast-moving predators looking for other creatures to eat in your compost pile. Generally they aren't a problem, but they will make a meal out of a nice tasty earthworm if they can get it.

Centipedes are territorial and use a set of poison claws to capture, stun, or kill their prey. The venom that centipedes possess is not sufficiently toxic to kill a human, but people who have handled centipedes report they can inflict a very painful bite.

If you think that the creatures are pests, the best method of eradication is to dose them with a bit of soda water to stun them, and then kill them with a garden tool.

Enchytraeid worms

These are also known as pot or white worms. They are relatives of the earthworm and are often mistaken for insect larvae in the compost pile.

Enchytraeid worms can be found anywhere earthworms are found, and like earthworms eat decomposing plant material. They are beneficial in your compost pile and help turn your plant material into wonderful nutrient-rich castings.

Flies

Flies are generally a fact of life when any decomposing is going on. They are always on the lookout for material to lay their eggs on. A fresh manure compost pile looks like the motherlode.

Adult flies themselves are a nuisance, but their larvae or maggots are what you will see burrowing in the compost pile. They are eating organic matter and converting it to basic nutrients, just as earthworms do. In this respect they are pretty good; the bad part is that your compost pile is playing host to thousands of new flies.

When dealing with compost piles on the ground, the best method of control—and this isn't a very good one—is to cover the pile with a tarp, newspaper, straw, or anything that won't allow the flies to lay eggs. Also try to bury new material deep in the middle of the pile to prevent flies from getting to it.

In a closed compost bin you have much better control over the problem because the bin is closed except for ventilation holes. Glue window screening over the holes to prevent the flies from getting in and laying eggs. Also, never place any food that has maggots in it in your compost bin. If maggots become a big problem, then stop adding material for a while. Without food, the maggots will either die or become adults and fly away.

Finally, you can trap away many flies that come to your compost bin. Find an old two-liter soda bottle. For fruit flies, add a solution of 1 cup apple cider vinegar with 1 or 2 drops of dishwashing liquid and set the bottle near the bin. For house flies, mix ½ cup apple cider vinegar with ½ cup water. Add a chunk of ground beef the size of a quarter. When bottles are full of drowned flies, throw them away and replace the solution.

Grubs

Grubs are beetles in the larval stage. They resemble C-shaped cocktail shrimp, and range in size from a half inch to two inches. Grubs feed on fresh plant material and break down the larger pieces into smaller pieces that can be eaten by worms and other organisms. In compost piles grubs are quite beneficial, but some people do not like the adult beetles they turn into. To keep the number of adult beetles down, toss large grubs out of the pile or bin. Birds will love the treat.

Millipedes

Millipedes look like large round segmented worms with lots of tiny legs. They eat organic plant material, just like earthworms and grubs. Millipedes are harmless. If you don't like them, hand-picking the slow-moving creatures out of the pile is easy.

Nematodes

These are slender round unsegmented worms that taper on both ends. There are more than 10,000 species of nematodes, and some are free-living while others are parasitic. Many nematodes are microscopic; some can be several inches long.

Many species of nematodes feed primarily on dead organic material and associated bacteria and fungi. These nematodes are an important part of the decomposition cycle and will be found in large numbers in any composting system.

Rodents

Rodents can sometimes be a problem in compost piles or bins. They are either looking for a nice warm place to live or for the tasty kitchen scraps you placed in the pile. To keep rodents out of bins make sure all holes or slats are covered with wire that has holes no bigger than ¼ inch. Unfortunately, there isn't a way to keep rodents out of piles on the ground. Try encouraging hawks in your area to keep rodent populations down (see page 150).

Springtails

These one- to three-millimeter-long creatures look like tiny white dots in your compost pile. If you try to touch them, they will spring away. Springtails are very beneficial in the production of soil humus and are considered an important soil organism. They feed on dead and decaying plant matter, fungi, and bacteria.

Planting, Potting, and Maintenance Solutions, and Some Tips on Tools

As much as people love gardening, sometimes it can be a lot of work. This chapter includes tips for making your gardening life a bit easier. We've included ideas for easy planting, weeding, and general garden maintenance. We will also show you how to make your own potting soil and grow great tomatoes.

QUICK TIPS FOR THE GARDEN

Gardeners pass lots of tips to each other. Here are some we've heard that we hope you may find helpful

ARTICHOKE TRANSPLANTS
Artichokes send up suckers that you can transplant. Simply remove the sucker, taking care not to damage the roots, and start a new plant.

ASPARAGUS WEEDS
To control weeds around asparagus, try putting down three to four inches of sawdust mulch from untreated wood. The sawdust discourages insects, but the asparagus can poke through easily. Sawdust can become matted down, so fluff periodically or mix with a coarser material. If you like white asparagus, heap soil or mulch around the spears so just the tips show.

BULB STORAGE

When digging up bulbs to be stored for next season's planting, sprinkle some medicated talcum powder on them before storing in order to prevent diseases.

CANTALOUPE PICKING

A good friend told us not to pick cantaloupes until the stem attaching the cantaloupe to the vine starts to dry out. Then the melon would be at its sweetest. He was right!

CUCUMBER CLIMBERS

Start your salad cucumbers in tomato cages. The vines grow up and the cucumbers hang down, making picking easier. In addition, you don't have to worry about ground rot.

GROWING MORE BEANS

To get a bigger production of beans, plant your beans next to sweet peas or morning glories. These plants fix nitrogen in the soil and the beans benefit from the added nitrogen. Peas and morning glories also attract pollinators early for added pollination success.

GROWING MORE CABBAGES

A neighbor discovered this successful trick. She grew cabbages and then harvested the heads but left the lower leaves attached to the roots of the plant. She continued to water the unsightly cabbage plants, and in a few weeks had more heads starting on them.

HEAVY SPRAYER?

Gardeners must often use a fairly large sprayer to reach the tops of their trees. These sprayers can be heavy when full. Try placing your sprayer in an old golf cart with wheels, making for easy pulling through the garden.

HERBS FOR DRYING

Growing herbs is so easy that you often end up with lots to dry. Here's an easy way to dry them. Place stripped leaves in a brown paper bag. Then shake the bag every few days to mix up the leaves and get air circulating. Of course, the old method of hanging herbs upside down to dry them works too. After drying, use some as air fresheners when you vacuum. Herbs such as lemon verbena, rosemary, or basil work well for this.

Just vacuum up about ⅓ cup of dried crushed herbs into the vacuum bag before doing the rest of your carpet. As you vacuum, the smell of herbs will fill the air.

HOMEMADE ROASTED SUNFLOWER SEEDS

Have you ever wanted to roast your own sunflower seeds? Here is a simple recipe. After harvesting, remove the seeds from the heads. Seeds that are ready for harvest are white and plump. Now soak the seeds in water for a week. If you like them salted, place one full pound of salt into enough water to cover the seeds. Make sure to keep the salt well dissolved in the water during the soaking period. After soaking, remove the seeds from the water, do not rinse, and spread them in a thin even layer on a cookie sheet. Place in the oven for 1 hour at 350 degrees. In about 45 minutes check for doneness. They are done when they just start to turn golden brown.

MELON CARE

To keep chewing insects from eating your melons before you harvest them, slip the unripe melons into one leg of a pair of pantyhose. Loosely tie the pantyhose on the stem end. Make sure there are no holes in the pantyhose that the insects can get through. This method also works well with corn, cabbages, grapes, cucumbers, peaches, and squash.

MINI PLANT COVERS

Make minigreenhouses. Cut the bottoms off clear two-liter plastic soft drink bottles and place the bottles over transplanted seedlings on cool nights.

PENNYROYAL TO CHASE PESTS

For an easy pest repellent for yourself or your pet, grow some pennyroyal in your garden. When you go outdoors, just pick a few leaves and rub them on your skin. Flying insects such as flies, mosquitoes, and gnats will stay away. Some people say pennyroyal repels ticks and chiggers too.

POLLINATING POINTERS

This is a great idea for those of you who have a fruit tree that needs cross-pollination but you don't have a second tree. The key is to find another tree and then ask the owner if you could trade some flowering branches.

Take the branches home and arrange them in a bucket filled with water. Make sure they are secure. Now tie the bucket in your tree. When bees come to pollinate your tree, they will cross-pollinate it with the flowering branches from the other tree at the same time.

POTATO SCAB PREVENTION

Pine needles placed in the bottom of a planting hole or trench can prevent scab on potatoes.

RETAINING SOIL MOISTURE

It is hard to keep the top layer of soil moist on windy days. Yet it is especially important to do so if you are sprouting a lawn or seedbed. To solve this problem, wet some burlap bags and place over the area that needs to stay moist. The burlap allows air to pass while keeping the top layer of soil moist.

ROSES AND SOIL

Roses like well-draining soil. To test if yours drains well, choose a nice sunny spot and then dig a hole about 1½ feet deep and 2 feet wide. Pour in at least 2 gallons of water. If it doesn't drain away in a few minutes, this may not be the best area for your rose. If it does drain well, plant the rose in the hole with equal parts soil, sand, and compost.

Many rose gardeners swear they get wonderful roses by adding Epsom salts to the bases of their rose bushes. Epsom salts, is high in magnesium. The usual dosage is ½ cup Epsom salts, around each bush in the spring. One note of caution: in areas with a lot of salt content in the soil, using Epsom salts is not recommended.

SHADING DELICATE VEGETABLES

Sunflowers will cast welcome shade over shade-loving vegetables like cucumbers and lettuce. But don't plant sunflowers too close to other plants because they can retard the growth of some. Growing corn to shade cabbage or spinach is another solution.

PLANTING TIPS

~ Sometimes small seeds are hard to see when planting. For better visibility, try mixing some white silica sand with the seeds when planting your rows or broadcasting wildflower seeds.

~ Marking off your garden can be a big job. Staking and running strings is one method, but the string can get in the way of planting. Try marking the garden or planting area off with flour. Use the flour as you would chalk to mark off a baseball diamond. Later, the flour will just wash away.

~ Cut planting time and use less space by planting crops that mature at different rates. Try planting radish seeds with other favorite vegetables, such as carrots or beets. The radishes will germinate first and will be almost ready to eat when the other vegetables sprout.

~ Plant lettuce between rows of other plants. The lettuce will benefit from the shade during summer and will take up less room in the garden.

~ When planting cucumbers, pumpkins, melons, and squash, the mounds and the area around the mounds may look a bit bare until the vines grow and spread. To save space, plant quick growing crops that will mature quickly around the mounds; try radishes, green beans, peas, and lettuce.

~ In colder climates, keeping the soil warm enough for early harvests can be a problem. Lay black plastic over your prepared bed and cut holes in it just large enough for planting and watering. The plastic will keep weeds down and help warm the soil. When the weather warms up, remove the plastic or just lay some mulch over it.

~ Planting seeds or seedlings in trenches instead of raised rows will direct the water to the plant and help protect the seedlings against drying winds.

~ Keep cutworms from chewing on new seedlings by wrapping a piece of newspaper, straw, or aluminum foil around the roots and stems of seedlings.

~ To save space in your garden, try planting corn with light vining crops like beans and peas. The corn stalks will support the vines and you will get two crops in the space of one.

~ To have vegetables throughout summer and fall (or until freezing weather), try staggered planting. Plant the vegetables every two weeks or so. Corn and tomatoes work well with this type of planting. As you finish eating the first planting, the second planting will be ready, then the third, and so on.

WATERING TIPS

~ Rather than simply watering hanging plants, use ice cubes. The ice cubes melt slowly so there is no gush of dripping water from the hanging plant.

~ Try misting wilted plants to revive them. Misting is great for stressed plants in hot weather. After the plant is well misted, water as usual.

~ Jug watering is great for slow watering. Punch a few holes in the bottom of a one-gallon plastic milk jug. The more holes, the faster the water will emerge; the fewer holes, the slower the trickle. Fill the jug and set it next to plants. The plants are then slowly watered, and no water splashes up on the plants to cause problems. Add liquid fertilizer to the jugs if you need to fertilize as well. Instead of a milk jug, you can substitute a large coffee can or a bucket, but if you do use open containers, take care that small children and pets don't get into them.

DON'T DEADHEAD FLOWERS AGAIN

If you are like us and love flowers but not the work that is necessary to maintain them, try planting one or more of these flowers that don't require you to snip dying heads off to look good.

~ Annual baby's-breath (*Gypsophila elegans*) is a bushy eighteen- to twenty-four-inch plant that puts out white or pink small flowers all summer long.

~ Baptista (*Baptista australis*), lunaria (*Lunaria annua*), love-in-a-mist (*Nigella damascena*), and blackberry lily (*Belamcanda chinensis*) all have decorative seed heads or pods that are quite attractive later on in the season.

~ Bearberry (*Arctostaphylos uva-ursi*) is a drought-resistant shrub that starts out in the spring with light pink flowers, turning later to red berries. The lovely evergreen foliage turns red in the fall. Bearberry likes any type of soil in sun or partial shade.

~ Brazilian vervain (*Verbena bonariensis*) is a tall annual that has tiny, pinkish lavender flowers. It is heat- and drought-resistant, and butterflies love it.

~ Bunchberry (*Cornus canadensis*) is a short ground cover that has white dogwood-like flowers that turn into red berries. It likes moist, acidic soil in shady areas.

~ Cascades mahonia (*Mahonia nervosa*) is a low-growing shrub with bright yellow flowers that bloom in eight-inch clusters in the spring and then turn into small blue fruit. It thrives in partial shade, well protected from wind.

~ Cleome (*Cleome hasslerana*) is a heat- and drought-tolerant plant with pink, magenta, or white flowers on three- to five-foot-tall stems. Butterflies and bees like this plant too.

~ Common yarrow (*Achillea millefolium*) produces pink or red flat-topped flowers that bloom all summer on two-foot stems. The plant looks dainty, but common yarrow is heat and drought resistant and spreads quickly.

~ Feverfew (*Chrysanthemum parthenium*) puts out white daisylike flowers on one- to three-foot-tall stems. Tolerates partial shade. The flowers attract beneficial insects.

~ Gaura (*Gaura lindheimeri*) are shrubby plants that put out lovely, delicate white to pink flowers on two- to three-foot stems. Once established, they are drought resistant and do well in the heat.

~ Heliotrope (*Heliotropium arborescens*) is a fragrant annual that puts out small purple or white flowers in tight groups on tall stems. It blooms from spring until late summer.

~ Kalimeris (*Kalimeris pinnatifida*) will give you beautiful white daisies with yellow centers from summer to fall. This is a good plant to try if you have moist soil in sun or partial shade.

~ Mealycup sage (*Salvia farinacea*) produces flower spikes of blue or white on a two- to four-foot-tall plant.

~ Pincushion flower (*Scabiosa caucasica*) is an eighteen-inch plant that puts out lots of lavender-blue flowers from late spring to the first good frost. Pincushions like well-draining soil in sun or partial shade.

~ Purple coneflower (*Echinacea purpurea*) is a drought-tolerant plant that puts out beautiful daisylike flowers from spring to fall. Seed heads make great bird food in the winter. Establish plants in full sun.

~ Russian sage (*Perovskia atriplicifolia*) is a shrubby plant that is covered in tiny blue flowers from midsummer to fall. Likes well-draining soils in full sun.

~ Snapdragon (*Antirrhinum majus*) comes in many varieties with flowers of many different colors. Plants range in size from a small seven inches to a tall three feet. Snapdragons like light shade and may need extra water in the heat of summer.

~ Threadleaf coreopsis (*Coreopsis verticillata*) provides a bounty of light yellow daisies from June through fall. Plants grow to be about one foot tall and spread by runners. Give them a sunny site.

~ Common bleeding heart (*Dicentra spectabilis*) and primroses are perennials that have a short growing season. The plants will fade away without necessitating much cleanup, leaving room for other later season flowers, like plumbagos.

USING EARTHWORMS TO MAKE GOOD TOPSOIL

It is estimated that in areas with large numbers of earthworms, the worms can cover an acre of land with as much as eighteen tons of new soil each year. However, it is also estimated that we are using seventeen times more topsoil than is being produced.

Have you ever wondered where topsoil comes from? In fact, earthworms make it, and they are the only organisms that can. They do this by eating leaves and other plant material and then depositing castings, or excrement, back into and at the surface of the soil. And, of course, earthworms are also essential to good soil composition.

How do you get these great soil builders to build more topsoil in your garden? Make your garden earthworm-friendly by doing some of the following:

~ Mulch the soil. Mulching adds organic material to the soil, which creates plenty of worm food and helps regulate soil temperature. These are ideal conditions for worms.

~ Leave the catcher off your mower. Like mulch, grass clippings provide food for earthworms. Clippings can raise the pH of your soil, so watch for that and if needed add a bit of garden lime or calcium carbonate to make the worms happy.

~ Add worms to a compost pile. Worms will generally migrate to a compost pile after the initial heating process. By adding some extra worms, you will improve the quality of your compost and have extra worms to spread in the garden along with it. These transplanted worms will have compost to eat and new garden soil to make. If you decide to add a lot of worms at one time to your garden, add at least two inches of good compost on top of the worms. Then apply another two inches every six months to keep the organic content high.

~ Fertilize the soil. Fertilizers added to the soil increase plant production and provide extra food for worms. Give your garden a good organic fertilizer, and let the old leaves fall and decompose for the worms.

~ Don't overtill the soil. Research show that soils that have been tilled frequently don't have as many worms as soils that have never been tilled. Earthworms are natural tillers, so let them do the work.

~ Keep soils moist. Earthworms need moist soils to breathe, so they will leave soils that are too dry. Keep the soil moist and encourage them to stay with plenty of food.

~ Add garden lime. Earthworms prefer a slightly alkaline soil, so if you have an acidic soil, an application of some garden lime or calcium carbonate will bring the soil up to the pH that earthworms love.

TIPS FOR THE CHRISTMAS SEASON

Here are tips for long-lasting Christmas trees and ever-blooming poinsettias.

KEEP YOUR CHRISTMAS TREE FRESH
Mix up this solution and soak your tree for a fresh tree all season. Be sure to do this outside, because bleach and carpets don't mix.

1 gallon warm water
1 pint clear corn syrup
4 ounces chlorine bleach
¼ teaspoon borax
2 ounces clear vinegar
2 ounces liquid detergent for delicate washables

Cut off the bottom 2 inches of the trunk. Mix together the ingredients and place the solution in a large bucket. Do this outside so as not to damage your carpets or floor with the bleach. Now place cut tree in the bucket and let the tree soak for 12 to 24 hours. Remove tree from solution and place in regular tree stand. Bring tree indoors and water with plain water as usual.

Note: Trees treated in this manner may require more water than those you've had in the past. Watch the water level carefully and do not let it dry out.

FLOWERING POINSETTIAS YEAR AFTER YEAR

Many of us enjoy poinsettias during the holidays, but afterward most plants end up in the compost pile or garbage can. This doesn't have to happen. You can have a beautiful poinsettia plant year after year. How?

First, remember three holidays: Easter, Independence Day, and Labor Day. These are the times at which you need to prune and feed your poinsettia. On each of these holidays prune the plant back, leaving four to six buds. Leave the plant in a bright place, but not in direct sunlight. Water the poinsettia when the soil first dries and give it a good all-purpose organic fertilizer.

During the first week of October, when the nights grow shorter, the plant needs to be in total darkness for a full fourteen hours every night. And we mean total darkness. Even a flash of light can ruin your chances of a good bloom. Try placing an appropriately sized cardboard carton over the plant at the same time every night. Continue this practice for eight to ten weeks. If you've done it all right, your poinsettia will develop a colorful display of blooms for the holidays!

How to Get Free Plants

There are many ways to obtain free plants. Some are obvious—saving seeds and dividing plants, for example—but in this section we offer a few other ideas as well.

DIVIDING

This is a great way to get two or more plants from just one plant. Most herbaceous plants that increase in size by forming new stems and roots can be divided. Dividing is great for most perennials and many types of bamboos, ferns, grasses, and herbs.

The best time to divide perennials that flower in mid to late summer—like asters, chrysanthemums, sunflowers, and Japanese anemones—is springtime. For those perennials that flower in spring, the best time to divide is late summer or early autumn. Some of these plants include peonies, columbine, bleeding heart, leopard's bane, and cranesbill. Divide clumps of bulbs about a month after flowering is over, when the foliage is dying back.

To divide plants, use a garden fork or trowel to gently loosen the clump of plants from the soil and lift it out. Knock off most of the soil and soak the clump in water to get a better view of where to divide it. Some plants can be easily pulled apart with your hands; others with stronger roots will need to be cut apart with a knife. Remove dry leaves, broken stems, dead roots, or pest-infested parts. Most clumps should only be divided into three or four pieces. Very small sections may be too weak to produce a healthy plant. Bulbs can be divided into as many bulbs as possible, but discard the small undersized ones.

Replant clumps immediately or store bulbs. Have holes or pots ready with fertilizer and good planting soil. It's important that the roots stay moist and don't dry out.

Ground covers are a snap to divide. Do you have a friend with an overgrown border of ground cover? Offer to divide it and have lots of plants for your own border.

Don't forget to divide houseplants too. Chinese evergreen, asparagus fern, arrowroot, and African violets are just a few plants that divide easily.

SAVING SEEDS

Saving seeds is almost as simple as letting a few plants go to seed each year and then collecting the seeds. Of course, nothing is *quite* that simple.

~ Don't save seeds from hybrids. You won't know what you'll get! The offspring from plant hybrids can be quite different.

~ Always harvest seeds from plants that are the healthiest and have the biggest blooms. Small, weak plants will produce inferior seeds, so pick nice big healthy plants to collect seeds from.

~ Seeds that are quite tiny in fruits or vegetables can be hard to harvest. Try this trick that works well on eggplants, peppers, and cherry tomatoes: Coarsely chop up fruit in a blender. Add water to cover. Blend until fruit is liquefied. Stop blender and let mixture sit until seeds settle to the bottom. If mixture is too thick, add more water. Pour off liquefied fruit and then pour seeds into a fine sieve. If seeds are very tiny, line sieve with cheesecloth or paper towel to collect. Dry seeds on wax paper.

~ For seeds such as those of tomato and cucumber, you need to remove the slimy coating before storing. Place the seeds in a plastic container with the lid ajar at room temperature for at least four days or until a mold develops on the seeds. Then rinse the seeds in a sieve to remove mold and coating. Dry on wax paper or a plate.

~ The seedpods of some plants contain chemicals that can irritate the skin. Okra is a prime example. So wear gloves when harvesting seedpods.

~ When picking seedpods or collecting seeds from native plants in nature, always leave some so the plant can reseed itself in its native habitat. Be sure never to pick anything in protected areas or national parks.

~ After picking seedpods, it's usually best to store the seeds in the pod until ready to use. Then open dried pods and pour out seeds. Always store seeds or pods in marked envelopes in a cool, dry place. Many gardeners also store seeds for next year's planting in plastic bags in the refrigerator.

~ Start roses from seeds. Yes, it can be done. Remember, seeds from hybrid roses will not breed true. However, you can save fully mature rose hips from nonhybrid roses for planting. When the hips are ready, the fleshy interior will be dry and you can slit the hips open and remove the seeds. Sometimes the whole hips are left intact and placed in cold storage, then the seed is removed before planting.

~ Treat seeds for fungus and bacteria. Fungus and bacterial diseases can ruin seeds. To kill the fungus and bacteria before storing, soak the seeds in hot water (at least 125 degrees) for thirty minutes. Remove and dry seeds.

Germinating saved seeds

~ Okay, you collected seeds only to find that many did not germinate when planted. An easy test for viability is to pour seeds into a glass filled with water. The seeds that fall to the bottom of the glass are good; throw away those that float to the top of the glass, or use them in a craft project. Another way to check viability is to take some of the seeds you've saved and place them between two pieces of moist paper toweling. Keep moist and check every day for germination. The percent of the seeds that germinate will correspond to the percent of viable seeds, so you can then plant accordingly.

~ Some seeds need a period of cold to emerge from dormancy. This process is called *stratification*. To do this, add seeds to a mixture of equal parts sand and moist peat moss in a plastic bag. Place the bag in a cold refrigerator (under 41 degrees) for four to twelve weeks before planting. Some of the plants that benefit from cold are aconite, bells of Ireland, bleeding heart, columbine, cotoneaster, daylily, euonymus, gas plant, hellebore, hickory, holly, juniper, lavender, lupine, peony, phlox, some roses, serviceberry, trillium, and violas.

~ Some seeds have seed coats that need to be penetrated in order to germinate. The process of breaking the seed coat to allow for better germination is called *scarification*. Nick a hole into the seed coat of large seeds with an emery board, sandpaper, or file. Soaking small seeds overnight in hot water (about 190 degrees) will achieve the same results. Just pour the hot water over the seeds and let sit. Don't do this until you are ready to plant the seeds since the seeds should not dry out before planting. A few plants that benefit from this treatment are apples, beans, beets, canna, carrots, celery, honey locust, impatiens, laburnum, lupine, mimosa, morning glory, pansy, parsley, peas, stone fruits, and sweet peas.

~ Start saved seeds by growing them in paper egg cartons. Fill the cups with sterile seed starting mix and add seeds. When ready to transplant, cut sections apart and plant the cup section with the seedling in it. The paper carton sections will degrade, and there will be less shock to the seedling.

~ Everyone knows about starting seeds between two pieces of moist paper toweling, but it's hard to start really big seeds that tend to dry out this way. Instead, slip the paper toweling and seeds into a plastic zip bag. Now place the bag in a warm area to allow the seeds to germinate.

DEADHEADING YOUR WAY TO BEAUTIFUL FREE FLOWERS

When you pull dead heads off your flowers, instead of throwing them in the compost pile, throw them into bare spots and cover with a bit of mulch or dirt. Before you know it the bare spot will be flourishing with flowering plants. Some flowers that grow easily from seed include zinnias, marigolds, bachelor's buttons, larkspurs, sweet peas, California poppies, cosmos, snapdragons, petunias, morning glories, and celosias.

WHAT TO DO WITH CUTTINGS

~ Take cuttings from your favorite annuals in the fall and root them in water or potting soil. Keep plants inside in a sunny spot like a bright kitchen window over the winter. In the spring you'll have plants ready for outdoors.

~ If rose bushes that don't have grafted root stock can grow in your area and are available, then you have a bounty of free roses. Ask your nursery if such roses are available. Then, when it is time to prune your roses you will have great cuttings to start a new bush just like the original one. To root the cuttings, place each one in a planting pot of about one gallon that is prepared with well-draining potting mixture. Keep the cuttings well watered and soon you'll have new rose bushes. Note that roses that have grafted root stock should not be propagated in this way.

USING SELF-SEEDING PLANTS

A good way to get more plants for your dollar is to buy self-seeding plants. When the plant dies at the end of the season it will leave behind seeds that will be ready to germinate next spring and take its place. Collecting seeds from a few flowers you let go to seed is another way to use the seeds from self-seeding plants. Just collect the seeds and broadcast them in various spots to increase the number of plants around your yard.

To promote self-seeding, avoid heavy rotary-tilling in areas where plants have died back and dropped their seeds in the spring. If the seeds get buried too deep, they may not germinate.

In the spring, don't put down mulch until the seedlings are up. Many seed varieties need bare ground and sunlight in order to germinate.

Talk to your local nursery staff. Ask for varieties of plants that self-seed in your area. You may be surprised to find quite a few plants—tomatoes, for example—that self-seed. Many native plants self-seed too. Don't forget to check these when planning a border or flower bed.

Here is a short list of flowering plants that self-seed. It will help you get started looking for the best ones for your needs. All of them are annuals, except for forget-me-nots, fringed bleeding heart, and honesty or money plant, which are biennials.

> Chinese forget-me-nots (Cynoglossum amabile)
> Cornflower (Centaurea cyanus)
> Cosmos (Cosmos bipinnatus)
> Feverfew (Chrysanthemum parthenium)
> Forget-me-nots (Myosotis alpestris)
> Fringed bleeding heart (Dicentra eximia)
> Garden balsam (Impatiens balsamina)
> Honesty or money plant (Lunaria)
> Love-in-a-mist (Nigella damascena)
> Marigolds (Calendula officinalis)
> Mignonette (Reseda odorata)
> Poppies (Papaver spp.)
> Rocket larkspur (Consolida ambigua)
> Sunflower (Helianthus annuus)
> Sweet alyssum (Lobularia maritama)

Here is a list of herbs that self-seed:

Borage	Chervil	Fennel
Calendula	Dill	Summer savory

MAKING YOUR OWN POTTING SOIL

Potting soil may be made of many different ingredients, so tailor-make the one that fits your needs best. Making your own potting soil not only is easy but can save you money.

MIX-AND-MATCH POTTING MIX

Potting soil usually contains 1 equal part of loamy topsoil, sphagnum moss, or peat moss, and 1 equal part of perlite, vermiculite, or sand. Other nutrients, such as compost and organic fertilizers, may also be added. Use the following ingredients to mix the perfect potting mix for you.

To make a basic potting mix, combine equal parts of one ingredient from column A with one ingredient from column B.

A	B
Loamy topsoil (soil that has a relatively equal balance of sand, silt, and clay and is also rich in organic matter)	Perlite (a granular, volcanic rock used to improve aeration)
Sphagnum moss (moisture-retaining moss found in bogs; low in nutrients)	Vermiculite (moisture-holding bits of expanded mica)
Peat moss (partially decayed sphagnum moss; low in nutrients)	Sand (fine rock particles, usually quartz, good for drainage)

Then add some of these to the basic mix:

Coffee grounds

Compost (use 1 part compost to every 4 parts potting mix)

Dried manure (use about 1 shovelful per 5 gallons of mix)

Organic fertilizers

Wood bark (use in large containers to keep soil mix loose)

Wood chips (use in smaller containers to hold water)

Worm castings or vermicompost (should make up from 5 percent to 25 percent of potting mix)

SPECIALIZED POTTING MIXES

Here are a few examples of potting mixes for specific needs.

~ Outdoor container mix: An easy mix for outdoor plants is 1 part loamy soil, 1 part compost, and a well-balanced organic fertilizer (use amount recommended on package for your container size and plant).

~ Propagating mixes: For root cuttings try peat, perlite, or sand as a base.

~ Quick-draining, lightweight mix: Good for hanging plants and others that need fast-draining soil. Mix 1 part loamy soil, 4 parts compost, and 4 parts perlite. Add appropriate organic fertilizer.

~ Seed-starting mixes: These are usually light, retain moisture well, and are sterilized to prevent fungal diseases. Try soil, sand, or peat mixed with vermiculite. These are usually low in nutrients. For example, mix 1 part vermiculite with 1 part compost, and sprinkle top with sand to discourage fungal diseases after planting seeds.

~ Soilless potting mixes: Try sphagnum or peat moss, perlite, or vermiculite alone or mixed together.

~ Worm castings mix: Make this balanced nutrient mix with 2 parts aged compost, 1 part castings, and ½ part vermiculite.

PLANT POTTING TIPS

Heavier soils hold more water and need less watering.

~ Plastic pots don't allow for water evaporation, and plants in them will need less water than those in clay pots. If you need the insulation factor that a clay pot gives, before planting line your plastic pot with newspaper or bubble wrap. Or plant in a plastic pot and then slip it inside a clay pot.

~ Mix small amounts of potting soil by shaking ingredients in a plastic bag. Use smaller sealed bags for leftover mix.

~ Use clothes dry sheets after they been used to line the bottom of a pot instead of stones. New coffee filters will also work, but why not recycle used ones in the garden?

~ To lighten heavy pots and use less potting mix, place styrofoam peanuts, pine cones, soda cans, or plastic bottles, among others, at the bottom of large pots. Put a piece of burlap or cheesecloth over them to make pot cleaning easier.

~ Not ready to repot, but think your potting mix has had it? Remove one or two inches of the old potting mix from the surface and replace it with fresh potting mix, mixed with a good fertilizer.

TOMATO MADNESS

Tomatoes are grown by more gardeners than any other vegetable. If the number of questions we receive about tomatoes is any indication, for some people it is the only vegetable to grow! But who can blame them? The taste of a fresh, homegrown, vine-ripened tomato just can't be beat.

GROWING TOMATOES

Growing tomatoes is not difficult, but it is not without its challenges either. To ensure you get the best-tasting tomato for your efforts, try a few of these simple growing tricks:

~ Grow the correct variety. This may sound obvious but it really isn't. How many gardeners do you know who have moved from one area of the country to another yet still try to grow that "greatest-tasting" tomato they remember from where they lived before? These gardeners order the seeds by mail or get them from friends and just "know" they will work. In the end, they are usually disappointed. Instead, go to your local nursery and ask which varieties do best in your area. Listen to the recommendations. Ask about diseases that might occur in your area and if resistant varieties are available.

~ Amend the soil. Tomatoes are heavy feeders. For an average bed of eight feet long and two and a half feet wide, we add one hundred pounds of compost and about one pound each of cottonseed meal, kelp meal, hoof and horn meal, and feather meal. Then we add two pounds of bonemeal and mix these fertilizers in six to eight inches. There is no benefit in placing the amendments too deep, because they will be carried down with the watering anyway. Finally, on top of the bed add a calcium source to prevent blossom end rot. Agricultural gypsum added to alkaline soil or dolomite added to acidic soil will work well. If your soil is deficient in magnesium, adding some Epsom salts will help.

~ Dig deep. Loosen the soil a good eighteen inches down. This will give your plants a head start in the race to grow healthy, deep roots.

~ Plant deep. You don't plant most plants any deeper than the soil level in the pot they came in. When planting pony packs of tomato seedlings, forget that rule—stick young tomatoes one or two inches deeper than the soil level in the pony pack.

~ Stake the plants. Growing tomatoes on stakes, trellises, or cages helps expose the leaves to the air and sunlight. This in turn helps prevent disease. Supporting the branches laden with tomatoes helps prevent the limbs from breaking off, too.

~ Water them. Tomatoes are best watered with drip irrigation or soaker hoses, which prevent the water from splashing onto the leaves and causing moist conditions for diseases such as mildew and late blight. Some gardeners water their plants with a bucket with holes punched in the bottom for a quick and easy drip method. (See page 106 for more on this method.) Don't overwater. A good soaking once a week or so is enough. Too much water discourages production. Overwatered tomatoes that do form usually taste watery.

~ Cover them. Tomatoes will not set fruit until nighttime temperatures stay above 55 degrees. To protect new plants from late frosts, place two-liter bottles with the bottoms cut off over seedlings. In very cool climates, it is best to keep a row cover on the plants. You can make a simple row cover by draping row cover material over stakes around plants. We know one gardener who places black stones (the kind used for decorative rock gardens) around her tomatoes. They absorb the heat of the sun during the day and keep the soil warm at night. Using old tires to ring growing tomatoes is basically the same idea.

BATTLING BIRDS AND SQUIRRELS

Many gardeners find that birds have pecked holes in their tomatoes or squirrels have nibbled on them. These creatures aren't tomato fans, but they do love the water inside them. Try placing a birdbath or other water source near your tomatoes and see if the damage stops. You can make an easy watering station from a tomato cage and plastic pot saucer. Push the tomato cage deep into the ground so it is stable, then place a plastic pot saucer on top. Make sure that the saucer fits securely. Fill with water.

Weeding Made Simple

Weeds are just plants growing in the wrong place. Homeowners and gardeners spend millions of dollars each year to rid gardens of weeds. The bottom line on weeds is, we keep spraying them and they keep coming back. Then all we have done is add more chemicals to the soil that can pollute our groundwater. What can we do?

SMOTHER WEEDS OUT

All plants need sunlight to live. If you block the sun, the plants soon die. Use this idea to smother weeds away. Place newspaper, cardboard (boxes that pizzas came in, for example), geotextiles (agriculture or landscaping cloth), or plastic over weeds. Top the newspaper or other material with bark chips or mulch so it looks more attractive. If you are using newspaper, wet the paper after you have put it down in order to keep it in place. Use six to twelve sheets for good light blockage. Cut holes in the layer of material and put in shrubs or vegetables. The area will be weed-free.

MULCH WEEDS OUT

Place at least three inches of wood chips, straw, shredded leaves, pine needles, compost, or other mulch over weeds to block out the sun completely. If you know your soil is alkaline or acidic, pick a mulch that will help neutralize the pH. Put down the mulch in the fall and you will have a weed-free area to plant in next spring.

You can also place mulch around existing plants to choke weeds from between plants. To prevent rot, don't let the mulch touch the plant's stem.

PLANT WEEDS OUT

Basically, you can plant anything as a cover crop if you plant it close enough together so that there is no bare ground. Try planting a cover crop of rye, clover, or buckwheat to control weeds. Many cover crops also attract beneficial insects, have showy flowers, and deter brushfires. Ground covers such as ice plant or lantana can also choke weeds out. Space ground cover plants twice as close as recommended. They will fill in faster, reducing the amount of bare ground and weeds. Ground covers usually don't mind dense plantings either.

CUT WEEDS OUT

Don't pull those weeds—just cut them. Repeated cuttings will eventually kill the weed by not allowing the leaf growth that produces food for the plant. Use a stirrup hoe or lawn mower to take off just the top of the weeds. Because you are not digging down into the soil, you will not bring up more weed seeds. A quick cut from a pocketknife on a lone weed works well too.

COOK WEEDS OUT

Soil solarization means letting the sun kill the weeds and their seeds for you. It is a great idea, but it does have a downside: it takes time.

Lay a piece of clear plastic over the weedy area. Anchor the plastic with bricks or stones on all sides. Then wait. The sun will heat the soil under the plastic and cook the weeds. In very hot areas, weeds may die in as little as three weeks; in cooler areas, the process can take up to two months or longer. The average is four to six weeks.

When it is time to remove the plastic don't till the soil. Tilling will bring up buried weed seeds that the heat didn't reach. Just rake lightly.

If you have plenty of time or many weeds, you may want to repeat the process. After the first heating, till the soil to bring up the buried weed seeds. Water the area to germinate. When the seeds start to sprout, replace the plastic and cook again for another four to six weeks.

If waiting that long is just too long, try tilling twice. After the plastic comes off the first time, till the soil, then water. Wait a couple of weeks for the buried weeds seeds to germinate. Then till again to kill the weeds that emerge. One note of caution: the soil solarization and tilling method of weed control is tough on earthworms, since they live in the top inches of the soil and don't like hot temperatures!

EAT WEEDS OUT

Some weeds are edible. Why not incorporate them into your next meal? You may like them so much you will plant some on purpose! Try the young tender greens in salads; leave the old bitter leaves on the plant. Of course, always double-check the plant identification with an expert before eating, and never eat any plant that may have been sprayed with insecticide.

Here's a list of a few edible weeds:

Chickweed greens	Nasturtium (petals)
Dandelion greens	Purslane
Lamb's quarters	Violet (leaves and flower petals)
Mustard greens	

SPRAY WEEDS OUT

Just like other plants, weeds cannot tolerate certain chemicals, including alcohol, vinegar, and soap. Use this knowledge to mix up a batch of cheap and easy weed killer. These sprays are similar to those we use to control pests and diseases, only much stronger.

Alcohol spray

2 to 5 tablespoons alcohol (2 tablespoons for little weeds, up to 5 for tougher weeds)

1 quart water

Mix ingredients together and pour into spray bottle. Mist the weed only; try to avoid other plants. Repeat if necessary.

Bleach spray

1 part bleach

1 part water

Mix the solution together and pour into a spray bottle. Mist weeds. This works on tough weeds, like those that grow in cracks in sidewalks and driveways. For really tough weeds, use bleach full-strength but keep well away from other plants.

Soap spray

6 tablespoons dishwashing liquid

1 quart water

Mix solution and pour into spray bottle. Spray weeds during heat of the day to allow soap to burn them. Repeat if necessary.

Vinegar spray

1 part vinegar
1 part water

Mix solution and pour into spray bottle. For tough weeds, use vinegar full strength, away from other plants. Vinegar spray works well on broad-leafed weeds.

Tips on spraying

When you spray weeds, be sure to spray the crown of the weed and not just the leaves. Never spray when it is windy. Make a shield from a piece of cardboard, to place between the weed and desired plants. Or make a spray dome for weeds. Cut the bottom off a two-liter plastic bottle. Place the bottle over the weed and spray down through the top. Cut a wider hole in the top if needed. You can use several sizes of bottles for all weed sizes.

BOIL WEEDS OUT

Pouring hot water on unwanted plants can cook and kill them. Be careful not to get the hot water on desired plants. Hot water works well on weeds that emerge from cracks in driveways and sidewalks.

SALT WEEDS OUT

Pour table salt on weeds that sprout in paved areas. Just make sure that the salt and its runoff does not come in contact with your favorite plants.

WATER WEEDS OUT

If you are desperate and just have to pull that weed, water it first to loosen the soil and make the weed easier to pull. Often, the whole root will come out with it.

KILL WEEDS BEFORE THEY EMERGE

There's something new on the preemergent herbicide market that not only stops weeds from germinating but also fertilizes the soil and is non-toxic. What is this marvel? Corn gluten meal, commonly used as a filler in dog food. You can purchase it by the bag from many mail-order garden suppliers, or ask your local nursery to order it.

The meal works only to prevent weeds (or other seeds) from germinating; it won't kill existing weeds. This makes it great at stopping weeds that tend to poke through lawns and bedding plants. As it breaks down, the gluten adds nitrogen to the soil. So don't add nitrogen fertilizer too soon after applying gluten meal. Wait at least two to four weeks.

WATCH THAT COMPOST—YOU MAY BE PLANTING WEEDS!

Many unwanted weeds end up in the compost pile. That's okay, but if the compost didn't heat up to at least 140 degrees, the weed seeds could be still be alive and germinate after the compost is spread. (See page 93 for tips on making compost.) Many gardeners have a separate compost pile just for weeds. That way, they are sure the seeds do not get mixed up with the compost being made for garden use. If you use compost you are not sure about or haven't bought certified weed-free compost, take two simple precautions.

~ Mulch over it. After putting down a layer of compost place a couple of inches of good mulch over it.

~ Bury it. Use this compost in deep planting holes and place dirt over it.

TOOLS THAT MAKE WORK EASY

When it comes to tools, most new gardeners think they are all alike. Well, we know that the pruning shears that fit the hand of one of us, who is 6 foot 3, sure won't fit the hand of the other, who is 5 foot 2. With the burgeoning popularity of gardening, manufacturers are customizing tools and making them easier to use.

RULES FOR PICKING THE RIGHT GARDEN TOOLS

Follow these rules for choosing garden tools that you will be happy with and use for many years to come.

Pick a tool that fits you

Check the weight, length, and grip to make sure you find the tool comfortable to use. Grips may be too large or small, and either can lead to blisters or cause you to tire easily. Some new pruners come with rotating handles; they make pruning easier on the wrist. Check the lock on the pruners, and make sure you can open and close them with your gloves on!

Buy high-quality tools

They may cost a bit more but you will save money and time in the long run. Often high-quality tools have newer designs that allow you to work more efficiently without tiring so quickly. Be open to new ideas.

Buy tools with forged blades

Tools forged from a single piece of steel instead of from folded or pressed steel are better. Look for loppers and hand pruners with heat-hardened steel blades. They are made to stay sharp and last. Tools are usually labeled: forged, drop-forged, or tempered.

Buy tools that can be taken apart and sharpened easily

Many pruning shears today have replaceable blades. Sharp tools make the work easier. Invest in a small sharpening stone or file to keep shovels and hoes sharp.

Buy tools with shock absorbers

They bear the brunt of each cut instead of your hands, arms, and shoulders. Padded or vinyl coated grips will also prevent blisters. Ash wood handles are better at absorbing shock than metal-handled loppers.

CLEANING TOOLS

Always clean your tools after using them. This can be as easy as wiping or hosing off the dirt and plunging the tool a few times into a small bucket that is filled with a mixture of fine sand and mineral oil. The sand will clean off leftover dirt and then deposit a light coat of oil to protect the metal from rusting. To make this kind of cleaning system, just place clean silica sand in a bucket and add about a cup of mineral oil on top. Mix the oil and sand together in the top few inches. Now plunge a pair of pruners or hedge clippers in. If the tool comes out with a light coat of oil, the oil-sand mixture is perfect. As the oil moves down through the bucket, add more if necessary.

Thorough cleaning is even more important when you use your tools to cut out a diseased part of a plant. To prevent spreading the disease, a disinfectant cleaning is a must. Mix a 10 percent solution of bleach and water (1½ cups bleach to 1 gallon water) in a bucket and dip your tools in. This will kill most plant diseases, although experts say to double the strength when dealing with fireblight bacteria. Dipping tools in 3 percent hydrogen peroxide will also disinfect them, but it is more expensive than bleach. When cutting extremely diseased plants, it is a good idea to dip the cutting edges in the disinfecting solution after making each cut.

When the job is done and you've dipped your tools in the bleach and water, don't forget to plunge them into your bucket of sand and mineral oil to protect the blades from rusting.

FREE OR ALMOST-FREE TOOLS THAT WORK

~ To finely dust plants, use one leg of an old pair of pantyhose. Just drop in the dusting substance and shake the leg up and down to distribute a very fine dust. Of course, when dusting always wear a dust mask.

~ Plastic pots make a great granular fertilizer spreader in tight areas. Find two plastic pots—the kind with holes in the bottom—that fit together well. Use old or new pots or even the plastic kind that nurseries use. Fit the two pots together so that the holes do not line up. Fill with fertilizer or other material. When you are ready to distribute the fertilizer, twist the pots so that the holes line up, then shake to distribute. Open the holes a lot to release a large amount; open just slightly to release a trickle.

Wildlife Loves an Organic Garden

Whether you plan for wildlife in your backyard garden or not, it is bound to be attracted by the wonderful pesticide-free environment you have created. Many gardeners welcome wildlife including butterflies, birds, and crawling creatures as an added bonus. They even plant trees and bushes that they know will send out the "welcome mat" for many species of animals. Such plantings increase the habitat available to animals as unpopulated natural space continues to shrink. The animals sharing your space can be just as prized as that beautiful red tomato you'd rather save for yourself.

This chapter will give some tips on how to attract many types of wildlife by creating a habitat and growing plants that animals need for food or shelter. Many of the animals that you attract will help your garden by eating unwanted pests, pollinating flowers, or by creating some beautiful wildlife music. However, sometimes wildlife in your garden can become unwelcome. Here you'll also learn some steps that you can take to keep your garden the place you want it to be, pest and chemical free.

BUTTERFLY GARDENING, OR ATTRACTING FLYING FLOWERS

Butterfly watching, like bird watching, is a fast-growing pastime for many people, and the art of bringing these beautiful flying jewels into one's own backyard is growing even faster. Butterfly gardening means planting trees, shrubs, or flowers that either the butterfly caterpillar or adult can use for food. Butterflies are not only beautiful to watch, but beneficial as well, playing an important role in nature. They are an important food source for other animals like birds and lizards, as well as being important pollinators of many plants. Without the pollinating work of butterflies and other insects such as bees, our world would be without many of the fruits and vegetables we love.

Butterflies are highly sensitive to pesticides and toxins in the environment. The absence of butterflies in a habitat can be an indicator of a problem. When plants can no longer survive in polluted areas, butterflies can't survive either. However, when a habitat is healthy, butterflies will flourish and will be found fluttering from flower to flower.

Currently, naturalists are looking at ways to increase the numbers of butterflies by bringing back some of their lost habitat, one piece at a time. Through these efforts, we all benefit from butterflies' integral role in nature and we also have the pleasure of watching them in our backyards.

MAKING A GOOD BUTTERFLY GARDEN

To have a successful butterfly garden you must take the entire life cycle of butterflies into consideration. An adult butterfly's main goal is reproduction, and just planting nectar flowers won't necessarily lead to lots of butterflies to admire—the female adult not only looks for plants from which to sip nectar, but also plants on which to lay her eggs. When caterpillars emerge from eggs they will survive and grow by munching on their host plants. Don't be alarmed. Most host plants grow back quickly. Male adult butterflies on the other hand, besides looking for nectar, are out looking for females. Sounds pretty familiar, doesn't it? So successful butterfly gardeners not only plant host and nectar plants, but also perches for males.

Your butterfly garden can be any size, from a window box to your entire backyard. Once you have determined what kinds of plants will work best to attract the butterflies in your area, use the tips below to make your butterfly garden as successful as possible.

~ *Start your butterfly garden in an area that is protected from the wind.* You may need to plant some barrier plants to break the wind if you live in a particularly windy area.

~ *Plant flowers that will bloom and provide nectar throughout the spring, summer, and fall seasons.* Perennials and long-blooming annuals will help ensure a steady supply of nectar. Try not to purchase nectar plants that have been heavily hybridized to create double flowers; usually these are poor nectar producers. Butterflies also seem to prefer brightly colored flowers. Their favorite colors in order are red, orange, purple, pink, blue, and white. It is also better to plant flowers of similar color hues together, instead of mixing colors together.

~ *Plant good nectar plants in the sun.* They should receive full sun from mid-morning to mid-afternoon. Butterfly adults generally feed only in the sun.

~ *Provide sunning or basking spots.* Butterflies are cold-blooded and they like nice warm areas to sun themselves. They fly best in temperatures between 75 and 90 degrees F. When temperatures are cool, butterflies will seek out areas with low ground covers, grasses, clovers, or light-colored rocks. When temperatures are over 90 degrees, butterflies will seek shade.

~ *Provide water.* Using a birdbath or other shallow container, place stones in the bottom of the container and add just enough water to come to the top edge of the stones. The stones give the butterfly a place to land without getting wet—a low spot in your garden that stays wet can also be used. Butterflies are often seen drinking next to muddy or sandy spots near streams and pools. This behavior is called "puddling." The butterflies love the extra salts and nutrients that are found next to puddles. Some butterflies require these extra nutrients to mate successfully. The nutrients are then passed from male to female during mating, so often more males will be found around puddles than females.

~ *Vary the environment.* The more types of habitat you have in your garden, the more species of butterflies you will attract. Habitats frequented by butterflies include boggy areas, shady wooded areas, woodland edges, sunny meadows, grassy areas, flower beds, and borders.

~ *Provide perching spots for males.* Many species of males including swallowtails and admirals like to perch on tall plants in areas where females are likely to be. Plant some taller flowers or shrubs near watering areas or near nectar and caterpillar host plants. Many butterflies like to perch in trees as well.

~ *Do not use insecticides of any kind near your butterfly garden.* Try biological controls if you need insect control.

A BUTTERFLY'S METAMORPHIC LIFE CYCLE

Butterflies and moths belong to the insect order *Lepidoptera*, meaning "scaled wing," which refers to the scales found on the wings of adults. There are over 125,000 different species of butterflies and moths in the world, and of these only about 12,000 live in North America. Butterflies only make up about 8 percent of all the lepidopteran species. Moths are much more common. Most butterflies are day fliers and are brightly colored, whereas most moths are night fliers and tend to be brown or dull-colored.

Most adult butterflies live only ten to twenty days, but the overwintering adult monarch butterfly can live up to six months.

Butterflies have what is called "complete metamorphosis." This means that there are four separate stages to their development: egg, larvae or caterpillar, pupa (chrysalis), and adult winged butterfly.

To start the life cycle, adult females lay eggs on or near a food source (host plant) that the newly hatched caterpillar will feed upon. The caterpillar resembles a tiny worm, but unlike worms they have a well-developed head, a three-segmented thorax usually bearing three pairs of legs, and a long, cylindrical abdomen of eleven segments. Caterpillars have chewing mouthparts and most feed on plant matter, while a few eat dried animal matter, and still fewer are predators.

Caterpillars will feed and grow rapidly, shedding their skins (or molting) four or five times before reaching full size. Some caterpillars are elaborately colored and patterned, while others are plain looking. There are also those that are grotesquely shaped or decorated with hairs, warts, humps, spines, or projections of all kinds, but for the most part they lack any defense mechanisms. A few do have poison glands or stinging hairs, and when handled or startled some can give off a repellent odor or fluid.

A caterpillar may increase its body size more than 30,000 times from the time it hatches to the time it pupates.

When a butterfly caterpillar has reached full size the next stage of life begins, the pupal stage. At this time the caterpillar will begin its transformation into a butterfly. The caterpillar stops feeding and looks for a place to hang from, then molts for the last time. During this molt a different skin is revealed that hardens and becomes the pupal case, or *chrysalis*. A chrysalis can be brightly colored and is usually attached to the larval food plant or some nearby protective support. Inside the chrysalis the caterpillar's tissues break down and reorganize into the structure of the adult butterfly. Moth caterpillars also pupate, but instead of molting in a chrysalis they use their modified salivary glands and spin a silken *cocoon* or build a leaf shelter in which to pupate. Many butterfly and moth species actually hibernate through the winter (or overwinter) in this pupal stage.

Finally, the butterfly will emerge from the chrysalis. It will have a fat body and soft, wrinkled wings. The butterfly will pump body fluids into the wings to expand them. After the wings have fully expanded and dried, the new adult butterfly is ready to fly, find a mate, and lay or fertilize eggs, thus repeating the life cycle.

BUTTERFLY FOOD REQUIREMENTS

Rather than the chewing mouthparts of immature caterpillars, adult butterflies have sucking mouthparts. The mouthparts are shaped into a long coiled tube, called a *proboscis*. The adult butterfly can uncoil its proboscis and use it to suck up nectar or tree sap. Plants that adults use for food are called nectar plants. Some adult butterflies and moths have reduced or no mouthparts at all and only live long enough to reproduce before dying.

Caterpillars or larvae use their chewing mouthparts to eat the leaves and stems of plant, called host plants. Some larvae, like the gypsy moths that feed in great numbers, can completely defoliate a mature host plant in a matter of days.

Many butterflies have very specific food requirements. Often the host plant for the caterpillar isn't the same nectar plant for the adult butterfly of the same species. To be a successful butterfly gardener you must provide both the host and nectar plants that the butterfly species in your area prefer to eat. If you are not sure what butterflies are native to your area, consult your local agricultural extension office, natural history museum, college, or a butterfly field guide. You can also watch your neighborhood park, creek, weed patches, or meadow and see which butterflies are flying around. Are they feeding on any plants? Can you find any caterpillars on the plant?

Planting native plants in your garden is a great way to attract butterflies. Check your local yellow pages for a Native Plant Society in your area. Usually they know which butterflies will be attracted to each plant, and often have plants available for sale.

The lists below give some examples of common host plants for caterpillars and nectar plants for butterflies throughout the United States. Ask your local nursery staff which ones are best suited for your area and climate.

Common Host Plants for Caterpillars

Alder	Coast live oak	Passion vine
Anise	Cottonwood	Plantain
Aspen	False indigo	Plum
Aster	Fennel	Pipevine
Apple	Grasses	Poplar
Baby's tears	Hackberry	Sassafras
Buckthorns	Hollyhock	Sedges
Cabbage	Hops	Snapdragon
Canyon live oak	Lilac	Spicebush
Carrot	Mallow	Sunflower
Ceanothus	Milkweed	Verbena
Cherry	Nasturtium	Violet
Citrus	Nettle	Wild senna
Clover	Parsley	Willow

Common Nectar Plants for Adults

Anise	Daylily	Mustard
Aster	Dogbane	Nasturtium
Bee balm	Echium	Oregano
Black-eyed susan	Firebush	Parsley
Blazing stars	Fleabane	Passion vine
Buckwheat	Heliotrope	Peppergrass
Buddleia	Hibiscus	Phlox
(or butterfly bush)	Hollyhock	Purple coneflower
Butterfly weed	Honeysuckle	Queen Anne's lace
Cardinal-flower	Impatiens	Sumac
Carrot	Joe-pye weed	Sunflower
Cassia	Lantana	Sweet pepperbush
Chrysanthemum	Lavender	Sweet William
Clover	Lilac	Thistle
Coreopsis	Marigold	Verbena
Cosmos	Mexican flame vine	Violet
Daisy	Mint	Yarrow
		Zinnia

ARE BUTTERFLIES EVER HARMFUL
TO YOUR GARDEN?

Gardeners are often concerned about the well-being of their garden when they see lots of caterpillars chewing on their favorite plants. As discussed, caterpillars eat host plants and then transform into beautiful butterflies. However, while gardeners will generally tolerate the chewing of *butterfly* caterpillars, they don't care for the chewing of *moth* caterpillars. But how do you know the difference?

Unless you are very experienced at looking at different caterpillars, it is quite difficult to tell a future butterfly from a future moth. Even many trained entomologists must rear the caterpillars to adulthood to make an absolute identification. If you really want to know what caterpillar is eating your plants, you can rear them too. It's easy.

To rear butterflies or moths you will need to assemble the following items:

~ An aquarium or large wide-mouthed jar with either a screen or piece of cheesecloth to place over the top.

~ A container to hold the plant material for the caterpillar. This can be anything from a baby food jar to a small plastic container. Stretch plastic wrap over the top of the container and secure with tape or a rubber band. This will prevent the caterpillar from falling in the water and drowning. When you are ready to add plant material, poke a hole in the plastic wrap, then add water and the plant.

~ Host plant for the particular caterpillar you are raising—usually the plant you found the caterpillar on. Make sure it is fresh and replace when eaten or wilted.

~ Several small twigs or sticks to lean against the sides of the aquarium or jar.

~ Sand, soil, or moist paper toweling for caterpillars to pupate in.

To set up the aquarium or jar, first place the sand, soil, or several layers of moist paper toweling in the bottom. Place one or more containers with plant material and water in the jar. Lean twigs or sticks securely against the sides. Now add your caterpillar(s). If you are starting from eggs, allow them to hatch in a small jar, then transfer the young caterpillars to the rearing container.

Check caterpillars daily and add fresh plant material when needed. Caterpillars do not need to drink water since they get all they need from the plants. This is why it's important that you not let the plant material dry out. When changing plant material, break off the stem the caterpillar is currently on and add it to your fresh container. The caterpillar will climb onto the new plant to feed. Be sure to clean up caterpillar frass (droppings) to prevent mold.

When the caterpillar has reached full size, it will stop eating and look for a place to pupate. Moths will construct a cocoon and butterflies will construct a chrysalis. Moths usually pupate in the soil and butterfly caterpillars will often suspend their chrysalis from twigs, plant material, or the enclosure screen. If you only want to determine if your caterpillar is a moth or a butterfly, you can stop rearing it as this point. As soon as a caterpillar constructs a cocoon you know it's a moth. If it constructs a chrysalis, it's a butterfly. However, by completing the process you will be able to determine the exact type of butterfly you're raising.

During the pupal stage, the butterfly or moth does not eat or drink, but care should be taken to prevent it from drying out. A damp sponge added to the jar or aquarium, a light misting everyday, or a piece of plastic wrap over the top of the container will help keep the humidity up if needed. Do not overly wet the container or mold will grow, which can harm your pupae. You don't want to see water condensing and running down the sides of the container. Increasing the humidity allows the newly emerged adult time to expand its wings completely before they dry. Several days before the adult emerges, the pupa will darken and the chrysalis will become almost transparent, allowing you to see the adult inside.

When the adult has emerged and completely expanded its wings, it is time to take the butterfly outside to be released. It may rest awhile before flying away, or it may take off fairly rapidly. Be prepared; after the butterfly is released your job is done! Now, enjoy the beautiful flying jewel fluttering in your garden.

A couple of precautions

~ Most moth and butterfly caterpillars are harmless, but some with branched spines can cause a sting. Caterpillars with straight hairs or single spines are usually harmless.

~ Caterpillars usually don't like being handled very much. Transfer small, newly hatched caterpillars with a soft brush. Do not handle or shake a caterpillar that is molting (shedding its old skin) or when it is becoming a pupa or chrysalis. They are very susceptible to damage at these times.

COMMON BUTTERFLIES YOU'LL FIND IN YOUR GARDEN

Following is a list of the common name and geographic locales of fifty-six common butterflies in the United States. Each will gladly visit backyard habitats planted with the appropriate host and/or nectar plants.

Butterfly	Pacific Coast	Desert South-west	South East	High Plains	New England	Mid-west
BRUSH-FOOTED						
American painted lady	X	X	X	X	X	X
Baltimore checkerspot			X		X	
Buckeye	X	X	X		X	X
Eastern comma			X	X	X	X
Great spangled fritillary				X	X	X
Gulf fritillary	X	X	X			
Milbert's tortoise shell**	X			X	X	X
Mourning cloak**	X	X		X	X	X
Painted lady*	X	X	X	X	X	X
Pearl crescent		X	X	X	X	X
Question mark				X	X	X
Red admiral^	X	X	X	X	X	X
Red-spotted purple		X		X	X	X
Variable checkerspot**	X	X				
Variegated fritillary		X	X	X	X	X
Viceroy		X	X			
White admiral**				X	X	X
Zebra			X			
GOSSAMER WING						
American copper**					X	X
Brown elfin	X			X	X	X
Common blue	X	X				
Eastern tailed blue	X	X	X	X	X	X
Gray hairstreak	X	X	X	X	X	X
Great purple hairstreak	X	X	X		X	X
Harvester			X		X	
Marine blue	X	X				X
Silvery blue	X	X	X			
Spring azure	X	X	X	X	X	X
HACKBERRY						
Hackberry		X	X		X	

Butterfly	Pacific Coast	Desert South-West	South East	High Plains	New England	Mid-West
MILKWEED						
Monarch*	X	X	X	X	X	X
Queen		X	X			
SATYRS						
Little wood satyr			X	X	X	X
Wood nymph	X		X	X	X	X
SKIPPERS						
Common checkered	X	X	X	X	X	X
Fiery	(CA)	X	X			X
Long-tailed	X		X		X	
Silver-spotted	X	X	X	X	X	X
Tawny-edged		X	X	X	X	X
SNOUT						
Common snout			X	X	X	X
SWALLOWTAILS						
Anise	X			X		
Eastern black	X	X			X	X
Giant		X	X			X
Pipevine	X	X	X		X	X
Spicebush		X	X		X	X
Tiger		X	X	X	X	X
Western tiger	X	X				
Zebra		X			X	X
WHITES AND SULFURS						
Cabbage white	X	X	X	X	X	X
Checkered white	X	X	X	X	X	X
Clouded sulphur	X	X	X	X	X	X
Cloudless giant sulphur		X	X			X
Falcate orangetip					X	X
Orange sulphur	X	X	X	X	X	X
Sara orangetip	X			X	X	X
Sleeply orange		X	X			X
Southern dogface	X	X	X			

*Denotes butterflies also found in Hawaii.
**Denotes butterflies also found in Alaska.

ANIMALS IN THE GARDEN

Most gardeners expect that animals such as birds, raccoons, and squirrels will come into their gardens. The allure of free food attracts both wanted and unwanted animals alike. However, many people go a step further and make their garden a wildlife refuge. They deliberately design areas of their garden to replace lost habitat land, knowing that all forms of wildlife from earthworms to bobcats may come. Such organic gardeners enjoy watching animals play out their roles in nature; by helping nature thrive gardeners ultimately benefit everyone. So by planting a small patch of land with native plants, a window box with a hummingbird's favorite flowers, or just hanging up a bird feeder a gardener creates a wildlife garden that improves our environment one piece at a time.

BASIC HABITAT PLAN

Creating a successful habitat area doesn't take much effort. Just keep in mind some of the ideas listed below when planting, and you will have lots of wildlife to enjoy.

~ *Diversity of plants.* Large flowerbeds of single flowers such as tulips look dynamic, but they aren't good for wildlife. Instead, plant many different kinds of plants with lots of natives in the mix. Plant trees, shrubs, flowers, and ground covers that will provide food and shelter the entire year.

~ *Make diverse habitats.* Think of layers when landscaping your yard. Ground layers might consist of a pond, a grassy area, a rock for basking, or even dead leaves left under trees for mulch or wildflowers. Upper layers could be anything from shrubs for shelter to trees for birds to roost in.

~ *Shade and light.* Make sure there are places in your yard that have shade and lots of sunshine. Nature is a balance, so plant trees and flowers that will give varied light to your yard. This will also help you attract reptiles, which need to regulate their body temperature by moving between shady and sunny spots.

~ *Water.* Every plant and animal needs water, and having a water source in your natural space is a good way to encourage all forms of wildlife.

~ *Do not use chemicals.* Certain pesticides and insecticides are deadly to wildlife. Instead of chemicals, learn to use natural pest control measures, beneficial insects, mulches, and other techniques to control pests and weeds.

BIRDS

Many gardeners have a love/hate relationship with birds. They love that birds eat pest insects, build nests, rear their young, and bring their melodic voices into the garden. However, gardeners hate birds when they eat prized fruit or vegetables.

Just like butterflies, birds have a definite place in nature. Birds eat insects and plants, and in turn become food for other animals. They also disperse seeds and keep many insect populations in check.

Most birds that visit your garden can be grouped by what they eat: insects, seeds, or prey. So some birds will be drawn to the garden to eat the aphids on a tomato plant, some to eat the seeds of a sunflower, and still others to eat rodents that are also looking for free food. By allowing birds to share your garden, or by planting their favorite plants, you increase the survival rate of birds in your area and allow them to continue their good work.

A LITTLE BIRD BIOLOGY

Birds belong to the class *Aves*, which includes about 8,600 different species of birds worldwide. Birds can be found in virtually every habitat in the world, from the polar regions to rain forests, from deserts to open seas. Birds can actually be found in more places in the world than humans, and have adapted to live in some of the harshest environments.

Specialized bodies

The anatomy of birds reflects the fact that they have adapted to living in every habitat and to feeding on many different types of food. While birds range greatly in size from the tiny hummingbird to the giant ostrich, they all share common characteristics.

- ~ All are warm-blooded.
- ~ All have feathers.
- ~ All lay eggs.
- ~ All have wings (though some cannot fly).
- ~ All have beaks or bills made out of a hornlike material.
- ~ All have scaled feet and legs.
- ~ All have hollow bones (though some are more hollow than others).

To compensate for their various habitats and functions, birds vary in the following characteristics:

~ Size

~ Shape

~ Coloration

~ Bill size and function

~ Wings

~ Feet

BIRD BEHAVIOR

Most of the fun of having birds in your backyard is watching their antics. By watching birds carefully, you will start to understand their unspoken language. Continued observation will also help you identify the specific species that have come to your garden or feeder. A few behaviors to look for are:

~ *Courtship rituals.* These displays by males toward females in the spring ensure that each species will survive. Females pick males with the fanciest plumage, prettiest song, best dance, and so on. Only males that are in peak form get a chance to mate. Look for males posturing or flying intricate patterns around females. Often the females will look uninterested.

~ *Territorial displays.* Males will defend and protect their territory from intruders. Sometimes a fight will erupt between two males. A territory may include a food or water source or a nest site.

~ *Defending young.* Some female and male birds have strong parenting instincts—you can see them defending a nest full of chicks. Female killdeers will often fake a broken wing to draw animals or other birds away from its young or nest.

~ *Young learning to feed themselves.* Watching a mother bird help her young learn to fend for themselves is a wonderful sight. When a fledgling is ready to be weaned, the mother will take it to a feeder, but initially the baby will want no part of feeding itself. The baby bird will continue to beg for food. The mother must teach by example, and the baby will soon learn how an adult bird feeds itself. Flying is taught in much the same way—by example.

- *Mobbing.* Birds stick together, and you'll often see a group of birds harass and chase a predator, such as a hawk, until it flies away from their area.

- *General hygiene.* All birds must take care of themselves. Some behaviors you'll see might include bathing, preening feathers, fluffing feathers, or dusting themselves.

- *Searching for food.* Every bird's survival depends on food. Some birds may scratch the ground looking for insects, others search for seeds or fruit. Even watching birds at a feeder can be quite interesting.

- *Nest building.* Females and some males build nests. A few birds like the killdeer just lay their eggs in depressions in the ground. Some nests are very elaborate, such as orioles', while others, such as doves', are simply a few twigs placed together.

- *Migration flights.* Who hasn't marveled at the "V" shaped formations of geese as they fly south? Many birds will stop along the way to visit feeders and water sources.

THE SPOKEN LANGUAGE—BIRD SONGS

The sound of birds singing in the morning is one of those extra pleasures a gardener gets. To people, singing birds usually signal that spring is in the air, but singing is much more than that to birds.

Birds sing and call as a way of communicating with each other. Each song and call has its own meaning. Good bird watchers know many of these sounds and can identify birds by their calls long before the bird is visually spotted.

Male birds sing to attract a female mate. This is one way a female may pick a mate. Even after mating, a male bird may sing throughout the nesting season. Females may also join in the singing during this time. Male birds also sing to warn other males from entering their territory.

Short calls or chirps are a bird's everyday language. Each sound has a different meaning, from "Danger is near" to "I found some food." Every bird species has their own specific calls, but some birds are very good at mimicking other birds' calls or songs. Naturalists are not exactly sure why birds mimic, but one thought is that it enhances a male bird's song, making him more attractive to females.

COMMON PLANTS BIRDS LOVE FOR FOOD

Now that you have decided to plant a few plants that birds will like, you need to know what to plant. Let's start with a list of plants that many birds will find appealing. This is a good general list if you don't have a specific bird in mind that you want to attract. These plants provide either food, nectar, shelter, or a combination of the three. They are suitable for various climates, so check your local nursery or county extension as to their viability in your area. Plants that will attract hummingbirds are marked with an asterisk. As an added bonus, many of the nectar plants will also attract butterflies.

Bedding Plants

Bee balm (nectar)*

Black-eyed susan (seeds)

Columbines (nectar)*

Cosmos (seeds)

Foxglove (nectar)*

Iris (nectar)*

Lantana (nectar)*

Phlox (nectar)*

Purple coneflower (nectar/seeds)*

Snapdragons (nectar)*

Sunflower (seeds)

Zinnia (nectar/seeds)*

(Most annuals, if allowed to go to seed, make tasty treats for birds.)

Ground Covers/Vines

American bittersweet (seeds)

Cross vine (nectar)*

Firecracker vine (nectar)*

Grapes (fruit)

Honeysuckle (nectar)*

Snapdragon vine (nectar)*

Trumpet vine (nectar)*

Trees

Alder (seeds)

Ash (fruit/berries)

Birch (fruit/berries)

Black gum (fruit/berries)

Buckthorn (fruit/berries)

Cedar (fruit/berries)

Cherry (fruit)

Conifers (seeds/nuts)

Crabapple (fruit/berries)

Dogwood (fruit/berries)

Elm (fruit/berries)

Hackberry (fruit/berries)

Hawthorn (fruit/berries)

Hemlock (fruit/berries)

Juneberry (fruit/berries)

Magnolias (seeds/nuts)

Mountain ash (fruit/berries)

Mulberry (fruit/berries)

Oak (seeds/nuts)

Sassafras (fruit/berries)

Serviceberry (fruit/berries)

Sweet gum (seeds/nuts)

Tulip tree (nectar)*

Willow (nectar)*

(Birds love all kinds of fruit trees, too.)

Shrubs

Barberry (fruit/berries)

Bayberry (fruit/berries)

Bottlebrush (nectar)

Buckeye (seeds/nuts)

Chokeberry (fruit/berries)

Cotoneaster (fruit/berries)

Dogwood (fruit/berries)

Elderberry (fruit/berries)

Euonymus (seeds)

Firethorn or pyracantha (fruit/berries)

Fuchsia (nectar)*

Hibiscus (nectar)*

Holly (fruit/berries)

Honeysuckle (nectar)*

Indian paintbrush (nectar)*

Juniper (fruit/berries)

Octotillo (nectar)*

Privet (fruit/berries)

Rhododendron (nectar)*

Roses (fruit/berries)

Smooth and staghorn sumac (fruit/berries)

Spicebush (seeds/nuts)

Viburnum (fruit/berries)

WHAT TO FEED YOUR FAVORITE BACKYARD BIRDS

Many people don't know what to place in their bird feeder for their favorite birds. The chart below details the various foods you can use in your feeder to attract specific birds.

Bird	Thistle Seed	Cracked Corn	White Millet	Black oil Sunflower Seeds	Sunflower Seeds	Beef Suet	Fruit	Sugar Water
American goldfinch	x	x	x	x	x			
American robin							x	
American tree sparrow	x	x	x		x			
Anna's hummingbird*							x	
Baltimore oriole							x	x
Black-capped chickadee	x			x	x	x		
Black-headed grosbeak			x	x				
Blue jay		x		x	x	x	x	
Broad-tailed hummingbird								x
Brown thrasher								x

Bird	Thistle Seed	Cracked Corn	White Millet	Black Oil Sunflower Seeds	Sunflower Seeds	Beef Suet	Fruit	Sugar Water
Canada goose		X						
Carolina wren							X	
Cedar waxwing								X
Chipping sparrow	X	X	X		X			
Dark-eyed junco	X	X	X	X	X			
Eastern bluebird							X	
Eastern towhee	X	X	X	X	X			
Evening grosbeak		X	X	X	X			
Gray catbird							X	
House finch		X	X	X	X		X	
House sparrow	X	X	X	X	X			
Indigo bunting	X				X			
Northern bobwhite		X	X		X			
Northern cardinal		X	X	X	X		X	
Northern mockingbird						X		
Mallard duck		X						
Mourning dove	X	X	X	X	X			
Pine sisken	X	X	X	X	X			
Purple finch	X	X	X	X	X			
Red-winged blackbird	X		X	X				
Ring-necked pheasant		X	X		X			
Rose-breasted grosbeak			X	X				
Ruby-throated hummingbird*						X		X
Scarlet tanager							X	X
Scrub jay		X		X	X	X	X	
Song sparrow	X	X	X		X			
Tufted titmouse	X			X	X	X	X	
Western tanager							X	X
White-breasted nuthatch			X	X	X			

Bird	THISTLE SEED	CRACKED CORN	WHITE MILLET	BLACK OIL SUNFLOWER SEEDS	SUNFLOWER SEEDS	BEEF SUET	FRUIT	SUGAR WATER
White-crowned sparrow	X	X	X	X	X			
White-throated sparrow	X	X	X	X	X			
Wood thrush							X	
Woodpeckers					X	X	X	X

*To make a sugar water formula for hummingbirds, mix 4 parts hot water with 1 part white sugar. Dissolve the sugar in the water and let cool before filling your feeder. Do not boil the solution. In addition, do not use red food coloring in your feeder because it isn't good for the birds. Instead, buy or paint feeders with red flowers to attract the birds.

Feeder success

Feeding birds can be quite simple, but certain problems do arise that you can ward off with these ideas:

~ Keep feeders clean to prevent diseases. Use soap and water or a weak bleach solution to scrub your feeder.

~ Clean suet feeders, too. They can become rancid in warm weather.

~ Don't place suet feeder in direct sunlight.

~ Clean hummingbird feeders every time you add the sugar and water solution. They should be cleaned at least once a week and more if it is very hot.

~ If you think the food has spoiled, dump it and clean the feeder.

~ Don't place feeders where birds could mistakenly fly into windows.

~ Place feeders near some sort of cover for protection, even within twenty feet will work.

~ If you like to use peanut butter, mix some cornmeal or other grain with it so it isn't so sticky. Try 1 part peanut butter with 6 parts cornmeal.

~ Use the right feeder for the right seed and the right bird. For small birds use a small feeder that will discourage large birds from using it.

~ Avoid overfeeding. Put out only enough food for the birds to use in one day.

~ In winter, place your feeder on the south side of your house. It will be warmer there.

~ If you are leaving on vacation or taking down your feeder for the winter, gradually wean the birds from the feeder—don't just take it down all at once. Decrease the amount of food in the feeder over several weeks.

~ Feed birds in the winter, especially when the weather is really bad. You'll help the birds get through until conditions improve and they can find natural foods again.

~ Provide water with your feeder, even in the winter. Electric elements for birdbaths work great for this purpose.

~ Finally, be patient. Sometimes it takes quite awhile for a bird to find and start using a feeder regularly. But the rewards are worth the wait!

PROTECT YOUR FEEDER FROM PESTS AND PREDATORS

Expect unwanted guests when you start feeding birds. Predators and pests are looking for a free meal, and will either find it in your feeder or make a meal out of the birds themselves.

Hawks

To help keep your new backyard friends from becoming a meal to a hawk or kestrel try one of these steps. Do remember that it is illegal in the United States to kill, trap, or harass native raptors (hawks, eagles, or owls).

~ Place your feeder near a tree or shrub that will provide dense cover if a bird needs to make a quick retreat from a predator. Many people actually hang their feeders from tree branches to give the birds a feeling of security by hiding the birds while feeding.

~ Feed the birds early in the morning. Hawks and kestrels are more often seen later in the morning and early in the evening.

Cats

Cats alone cause the death of more songbirds than any other animal. If you're having a problem with wild, or feral, cats, they can be live-caught and moved from the area. Generally feral cats hunt only at night and their main prey is mice and other rodents, so domesticated cats usually do the most damage to songbird populations. Tame cats have quit their nocturnal ways and become adapted to being active during the day, when songbirds are vulnerable.

Discouraging cats from chasing and killing birds is almost impossible, but you can give birds a better chance at survival by trying a few of these tips:

~ Convince neighbors who allow their cats outdoors to hang a small bell on the cat's collar.

~ Remove hiding places for cats to strike from—usually low dense shrubs. Alternatively, you could plant thorny shrubs that the cats are less likely to hide in.

~ Don't hang a bird feeder on a fence where cats can get to it.

~ If you have a tree in your yard, remove low branches that cats can pounce from. And be sure to cut back limbs that allow cats access to your yard.

~ To keep cats from climbing feeder poles, tie cut rose stems or thorny bushes to the pole.

~ Ask your neighbors to keep their cats in until midmorning and feed the birds early. This will allow the birds time to eat and leave before the cat is out.

Squirrels

Squirrels just love bird feeders and the seeds inside them, and are sometimes very hard to discourage. Some gardeners just give in and feed the squirrels too, making all the animals happy. However, if squirrels are too much of a bother to your feeder, try one of these ideas:

~ Slip cut two-liter soda bottles onto your feeder's pole. The slick plastic is hard to climb.

~ Place baffles underneath feeders.

~ Move feeders away from trees where a jumping squirrel can reach it.

~ Hang feeders from thick fishing line.

~ Hang a feeder from a clothesline that is strung with small pieces of PVC pipe. When the squirrel tries to walk on sections of pipe, they will spin, sending the squirrel to the ground. This idea works well on support wires too.

~ Feed the birds early in the morning. This will give them a chance to eat before the squirrels are out and about.

- ~ Don't put too much food in the feeder at one time. The birds will eat all of the food in the morning and leave nothing for the squirrels in the afternoon.

- ~ Mix birdseed with cayenne pepper. It doesn't bother the birds, but the squirrels will hate it.

Other aggressive birds

Some birds like pigeons, starlings, house sparrows, and blackbirds will try to claim a feeder for themselves. This isn't good if you're trying to encourage local cardinals, for example. The best way to control unwanted guest birds is to remove the kind of food that is attracting them. Some people will limit a feeder to just a few kinds of seeds they know the wanted birds like and the unwanted don't. Use the seed guide earlier in this section to help you determine the desired seed combinations for the bird you are trying to encourage. Or try one of these ideas:

- ~ To deter pigeons, eliminate corn, chicken scratch, and grains from the feeder, and try to keep the area under the feeder clean.

- ~ Set up a separate feeder with foods the unwanted birds will be attracted to so they will leave your other feeder alone.

- ~ Little can be done to discourage large groups of blackbirds and starlings. It is probably best to just stop feeding the birds for awhile until the flocks leave the area.

AMPHIBIANS, REPTILES, AND MAMMALS

When most people think of animals, they think of furry mammals, but many types of animals would like to live in an organic garden. Each animal brings its own living requirements, so different types of gardens will attract different animals. Let's look at each type of animal separately to determine which ones will want to come and make your yard its home. Of course if you want to discourage a particular animal, you can make your yard unfriendly by knowing what it likes.

AMPHIBIANS

There are 3,000 different species of frogs, toads, salamanders, and newts living in the world today. Most members of this class of animals have moist skin, no scales or claws, and spend the early stages of their life cycle in water. To encourage these animals in your yard, a backyard pond or other water source is needed.

Amphibians are great insect eaters. One toad can eat between 10,000 and 20,000 insects per year. Talk about natural insect control! Toads don't need to live in water after they are hatched, as frogs do. Their skin is dry so they can live on land for extended periods of time. All a toad needs to survive nicely in your yard is shelter and a large saucer full of water. The shelter can be made of anything that will provide a fairly damp environment. A small cave in a rock garden or a clay pot turned upside-down and propped up on one side will provide an excellent home for a toad.

All amphibians are very susceptible to pesticide poisoning. Many amphibians actually breathe through the moist membranes of their skin, making them almost defenseless against chemicals. Be very careful with any toxic material near or around an amphibian's home or pond.

REPTILES

There are estimated to be about 6,000 snake, lizard, turtle, and tortoise species worldwide. Most gardeners never consider actually inviting a snake to live in their backyard, but they don't think twice about the occasional lizard or tortoise. Many reptiles are very beneficial and eat a great many insects and rodents that we would just as soon not have around. Kingsnakes, for example, will eat rattlesnakes. (In fact, rattlesnakes have been shown to be actually afraid of kingsnakes.) So if you live in rattlesnake country, having a resident kingsnake would be a good thing. Another good example of a beneficial reptile is the alligator lizard, which eats black widow spiders.

Making your yard reptile friendly is really quite simple. Reptiles are cold-blooded creatures and need to warm up each day. Provide basking rocks or a ledge near the garden where lizards and snakes can go to get warm. Turtles are mostly aquatic, whereas tortoises are land-dwelling, but both also like basking areas. Be sure to have a large, flat rock close to the surface of a pond for a turtle to crawl up on, or a clear sunny spot for a tortoise. Tortoises are mostly vegetarian, so plant a row of green leaf lettuce or a hibiscus plant just for your tortoise to eat. If you don't want them eating your plants, then set out some snacks of romaine lettuce (no iceberg lettuce), cooked carrots and sweet potatoes, hibiscus flowers, or chopped fruit. They will be very happy.

All reptiles like a good hiding place too. Grassy areas, a wild patch of flowers, clay pots turned over, or a small wooden box all make great shelters for many reptiles. Well-manicured yards will not be as attractive.

When the weather turns cold, reptiles will hibernate. Snakes look for a den, lizards look for cracks and crevices in rocks or wood, turtles and tortoises may dig themselves a hole or depression in the soil to wait out the cold weather. If you want to keep reptiles in your garden through the winter, it's important to provide such hibernation spots.

MAMMALS

There are about 4,000 different mammal species worldwide. Mammals like rabbits, squirrels, opossums, and maybe even a skunk or two are common backyard visitors. However, there are lots of other mammals that would love to make your yard their homes, including foxes, bobcats, gophers, deer, mice, and rats. Each animal has its own benefit to nature, from opossums that eat rodents to skunks that eat insects. They are all part of the food web and balance of nature.

A mammal will visit or live in your yard if it provides food, shelter, or a safe place to bear and raise their young. Some yards will only provide a few insects (food) for a roaming skunk. The skunk will simply stop by to eat and then leave, but many yards provide all of an animal's needs. When a yard meets all of an animal's requirements, you can have permanent residents, wanted or not.

When encouraging mammals to your yard, you must consider what is best for the animal in the long run, and of course its impact on your yard and garden. Here are a few questions we are often asked about mammals, along with our answers, that will help you decide if and how to encourage animals in your garden.

- ~ *Is it okay to feed a wild animal pet food or kitchen scraps?* No, it is not! You shouldn't feed wild animals because you end up supplying them with more food than they would be able to find on their own. Extra food encourages the animal to have many babies that will also be looking for dinner at your house. Pretty soon there are more animals than the land can support. Once you start feeding them, if you stop, they will surely starve or become a predator's next meal.

- ~ *Should you plant native plants to encourage wildlife?* Yes. By planting native plants you are adding habitat for wildlife. A natural habitat provides food and shelter for animals.

- ~ *What about providing a water source for animals, like a pond?* This is also a good idea. Water is a key element to any habitat.

- ~ *Can you encourage one mammal while discouraging others?* That depends on the mammal. It is fairly easy to encourage one animal while discouraging another if they occupy different habitats. For example, gophers occupy an underground habitat, while rabbits occupy an above-ground habitat.

However, the problem arises when two animals occupy the same habitat and one is definitely not wanted. This is why many people have such a problem with mice and rats; they love the same habitat people do. The best that can be done in such a situation is to try to identify and eliminate the thing that is attracting the unwanted animal to your yard. Think about the food or shelter sources you may be inadvertently providing.

~ *Can predators be encouraged in a backyard setting?* Predators depend on prey to live. Not many of us would encourage prey species to live in our yard just to give the predators something to eat. However, many predators, such as foxes, will have a home base when rearing young. If you decide you want your yard to be a home base for a predator, try creating secluded areas where a fox or bobcat could make their den. To encourage birds of prey, place a pole in your yard at least fifteen feet high for the birds to land on. Or remove the leaves from one tall branch, leaving it bare for the bird. If you invite predators into your garden, you can't blame them for preying on pets.

~ *Can you have backyard pets and encourage wildlife?* Probably the biggest deterrent to encouraging native wildlife to one's yard is a dog or cat. Dogs like to bark and chase anything that moves while cats enjoy stalking small creatures. The scent of dogs and cats will sometimes deter animals as well. To encourage wildlife, keep dogs and cats inside or penned in a side yard away from the area to which you're trying to attract wildlife. This will also prevent unfortunate encounters with animals such as skunks.

~ *What's the best thing I can do to encourage wildlife?* Plant habitat that will be undisturbed. This means to plant native plants in areas without a lot of human or pet disturbance.

WILDLIFE BEHAVIORS, OR "TALKING TO THE ANIMALS"

When we start paying attention to wildlife by watching their comings and goings, we soon realize that each animal is a complex organism. They may not speak in a language we understand but they are being understood by other animals of their species. Zookeepers learn to read the body language, vocalizations, and demeanor of the animals in their care. They know if an animal is looking for a mate, hungry, or not feeling well. You too can come to understand the animals that visit your yard or garden at this level.

Here are a few tips on watching animals and understanding what they are saying:

~ First, don't let animals see that you are watching. Once they get used to you, they probably won't mind that you are there, but in the beginning stay out of sight as much as you can. Use binoculars if you need to.

~ Do you see certain movements or vocalizations repeated? What happened to instigate the behavior? Often animals will call one another or give a warning if danger is near. For example, hummingbirds give a certain sound when they are trying to chase another hummingbird away from the feeder. Soon you will be able to tell what they are saying.

~ Fill a feeder or place out treats at the same time each day. The animal you are interested in observing will know to show up for the treat, and you can watch it up close.

~ Watch for certain stances from animals. Fence lizard stances say a lot—everything from "Get off of my rock" to "Come here, lizard cutie."

~ Note what happens when another animal comes in your yard. Male birds will often let female birds come to the feeder with them, but will chase away other males.

~ Once you have animals coming regularly, change one thing and watch what they do. Make a small change such as moving your feeder just a bit. Animals' reactions are sometimes very interesting. We heard about a zookeeper who was putting away the giraffes one night. She didn't notice when a quarter fell out of her pocket. As she moved the first giraffe, an eighteen-foot male, toward his bedroom, the giraffe just stopped. You guessed it! He saw that quarter and wouldn't step over it.

~ Let children keep a log of what they see the animals do. Usually there is a pecking order with birds. Can they spot the one who is on the bottom? Or the top?

~ Put out nesting materials for birds and animals. Watching mothers with babies is a sure way to see precise communication between animals.

WHEN WILDLIFE BECOME PESTS

Some animals, no matter how cute they are, cross the line from cute at a distance to pest in the garden. The lure of your beautiful garden with lots of delicious plants to eat is irresistible for most animals. Planning ahead can help you control the animal pests in your garden.

~ *Fortify areas that are off limits.* Plant areas around garden beds with thorny plants or hedges, such as roses, barberry, pyracantha, holly, or gooseberry. These deterrents make great "fences" around areas where you don't want to erect a real fence.

~ *Provide plants the "pests" are allowed to eat.* Try planting some extra squash or zucchini plants around the edges of your garden. These plants will attract the pests and deter them from raiding the more desired vegetables in the center.

~ *Use the sprinkler.* Deter animals from protected areas by having a sprinkler ready. Nothing surprises an unwanted guest more than a spraying of water. Sprinklers are now available with motion detectors, which are great for those nighttime guests.

~ *Use repellents.* An old trick that still works is to sprinkle ground pepper on plants that animals are nibbling on, or make the following repellent spray. If making a spray is too much trouble, try planting garlic around your favorite plants that hungry rabbits, gophers, squirrels, or voles nibble on. As an added benefit, many insect pests are repelled by garlic as well.

General purpose mammals repellent recipe

> *2 to 4 hot chili peppers (the hotter the better, such as habanero or serrano) or 2 tablespoons cayenne pepper*
> *4 cloves garlic*
> *1 quart water*

Mix all ingredients in a blender. Strain and use the mixture in a spray bottle or hand-held sprayer. Be sure to spray again after a rain.

~ *Make pests think a predator is after them.* Most plant-eating animals, such as rabbits, deer, and squirrels, are prey for some other animal. Dogs, cats, and humans are predator animals. To protect your yard and garden from being invaded by prey animals, make them think a predator is near. If you have a male dog, he probably takes care of this for you by marking his territory. One sniff will tell a prey animal to stay away. If you don't have a dog, borrow a friend's, or place kitty litter or hair from your last haircut around the perimeter of your yard. Gardeners that do not have access to a pet can even use human urine to mark out their territories. In some areas fox and wolf urine are available commercially in nurseries, but they can be fairly expensive. If you can't find them at a local nursery, many mail order catalogs carry them. Using scents works well, but remember that after a while the pests will figure out that a predator isn't around after all, and will become brave enough to raid your garden. Deer are especially smart at figuring this out. You can avoid this problem by switching between various scents so the pests don't become accustomed to any particular one.

Below you'll find some tips to deter specific animals from your garden. Remember that not all tips will work every time—if you keep trying new ideas, you may find the one that works for your specific animal problem.

BIRDS

~ One problem with birds is they love fruit trees. Try planting a couple of berry trees that birds can feast on so they leave your desired trees alone. Some good choices are mulberry, chokeberry, dogwood, and mountain ash. Be sure to plant them away from your fruit trees.

~ Placing netting on plants that birds are pecking is also good way to prevent them from eating your prized crop. To be effective, you must seal the netting by burying it in the ground or the birds will find a way in. Stake the netting away from the plant so the birds can't peck the fruit or vegetable through the netting.

~ Make birds think a hawk is near by placing a silhouette of a hawk in a big window or hanging from a tree. This can also keep birds from crashing into large windows.

Woodpeckers

~ Silhouettes hung in trees may also keep woodpeckers from pecking the tree.

~ Hang aluminum foil or brightly colored strips of plastic or cloth at least two to three feet long from trees to chase away the birds.

~ Loud music or a water sprinkler can also be effective at repelling woodpeckers. Turn the music or water on when the woodpecker begins pecking, and leave it on until the bird flies away.

CATS

~ To keep cats from digging in your garden, place rose or conifer trimmings between the rows. Cats do not like stepping on unsteady or prickly ground. You can take this idea one step further and lay down pieces of chicken wire or welded fencing around shrubs. You can even plant flowers in holes cut in wire, covering the wire with a thin layer of mulch. You won't see the wire but the cats will know it's there. These tricks will work for skunks as well.

~ String fishing line between six-inch-tall stakes over newly planted seedbeds. The line should crisscross the bed and not allow the cat to jump into bare sections.

~ Spread an inch or so of cocoa mulch throughout your garden. This natural mulch is comprised of the dried hulls of cocoa beans. It has a pleasant chocolate smell, and cats and snails hate it. Renew it twice a year.

~ Spray lemon juice in areas where cats are digging. Or try spreading chopped up lemon or grapefruit rinds over the area.

~ Sprinkle ground black or cayenne pepper in areas that are off limits.

DEER

~ Start by planting plants that deer don't like. Remember that in times of extreme hunger deer will eat just about anything, but the following plants won't be their first choice. Check your local nursery or cooperative extension for advice on the suitability of these plants in your area.

Bedding Plants

Aloe	Dahlia	Lamb's ears
Astilbe	Dead nettle	Lupine
Bee balm	Floss flower	Oriental poppy
Blanket flower	Forget-me-not	Pincushion flower
Bleeding heart	Foxglove	Purple coneflower
Candytuft	Gloriosa daisy	Red-hot poker
Catnip	Hyacinth	Verbena
Columbine	Iris	Yarrow
Daffodil		

Ground Covers / Trees / Shrubs

Ground Covers	Trees	Shrubs
Ajuga	Ash	Bottlebrush
Bittersweet	Beech	Boxwood
Bougainvillea	Conifers	Butterfly bush
English ivy	Ginkgo	Firethorn
Lantana	Hackberry	Flowering quince
Periwinkle	Honey locust	Holly
Sweet woodruff	Oak	Juniper
Wisteria		Lavender
		Lilac
		Viburnum

~ Lay pallets on the ground around large areas you want deer to stay out of. They do not like walking on or jumping over pallets.

~ Mix a paste of hot pepper powder and water and spread it on the trunks of trees that deer are chewing on. Great for protecting saplings, which deer particularly love.

~ Place garlic supplements in pill form (not garlic oil pills) around the garden and specific plants deer are fond of.

~ Soak thick pieces of cotton, like the ones from pill bottles, in garlic oil, or better yet, garlic extract, and hang in trees or place around the garden.

DOGS

~ Common rue (*Ruta graveolens*) planted in and around your garden will deter dogs. It is said that planting a rue plant next to tomato plants will also keep dogs from eating the ripe tomatoes. An added bonus is that many insect pests do not like rue either.

~ Try planting calendulas. Dogs don't like it and won't dig in it.

GOPHERS

~ When gopher holes first appear, soak rags with ammonia and place them in the holes covered with dirt. One smell of the ammonia and the gophers will retreat elsewhere. Another method that works well for gophers is making them think a predator is after them by placing pet droppings in their tunnels.

GROUNDHOGS

~ Treat groundhogs much as you would gophers since they are both burrowing and prey animals. Try placing ammonia soaked rags, dog feces, or used kitty litter in their burrows to discourage them.

~ Chicken wire fencing buried at least twelve inches down and extending twenty-four inches above the soil's surface can block groundhogs' advances toward your garden.

~ Bait groundhog traps with lettuce or their favorite vegetable from your garden.

~ Plant a trap crop, just like you would for insects. Place a patch of alfalfa or clover (or whatever else groundhogs particularly like in your garden) fifty feet away. Hopefully the groundhogs will find the trap crop and leave your garden alone.

~ Keep a wide border clear of hiding places around your garden. This makes groundhogs vulnerable to their predators, such as dogs, cats, and hawks.

RABBITS

~ To protect trees from the nibblings of rabbits (and mice) wrap the base of the trunk with aluminum foil.

~ Use blood meal on your lawn to keep rabbits from eating it. Blood meal is dried blood and smells like death to a rabbit. Generally blood meal should be reapplied after a rain. One warning: if you have a dog, don't use blood meal; dogs love it and will try to eat it. To protect your garden, place blood meal in cheesecloth bags and hang them around the perimeter or near specific plants.

~ Rabbits don't like to cross wide-open areas, so remove hiding places. They are a prey species and are vulnerable out in the open.

~ A fence constructed out of chicken wire should keep the rabbits out. Make sure the fence is secure to the ground so the rabbits can't get under it. You can do this by burying at least six inches of the fence underground.

~ Try placing some old shoes or work boots in the garden to make the rabbit think a human is around.

~ Use the third, fourth, and fifth ideas in the deer section—they also work well for rabbits.

RACCOONS

~ To keep raccoons out of fish ponds make sure the walls of the pond are straight, not slanted, and at least eighteen inches deep.

~ A motion detector hooked to a sprinkler makes a great deterrent for raccoons.

~ To keep raccoons from eating corn, place a couple of drops of hot pepper sauce near the silks a couple of weeks before harvesting. Or you can place a paper bag over the ear and fasten securely. Planting cucumbers around your corn patch will also deter raccoons.

~ Place rose cuttings around desired plants or lay down loose chicken wire.

RODENTS

~ Many burrowing rodents will not dig through a barrier of gravel. Create a narrow trench six to eight inches deep around your garden and fill it in with gravel.

~ Plant mint or sweet peas around—mice hate them. Strong smelling herbs might work well too.

SKUNKS

~ Skunks love to eat the grubs in your garden and yard and will dig up everything looking for them. Releasing beneficial nematodes on watered areas should take care of the grubs, thus giving the skunks nothing to dig for. (Armadillos will also dig for grubs.) Many of the ideas listed earlier for deterring cats work well for skunks as well.

~ The worst has happened and your pet has been sprayed by a skunk. What should you do now? Grab the tomato juice? No, keep these ingredients handy and when disaster strikes you will be ready. This formula really works!

1 cup 3 percent hydrogen peroxide
¼ cup baking soda
grease-cutting liquid dishwashing detergent

Mix the peroxide and baking soda together in a container. Slowly add the detergent until the mixture is the consistency of gravy. Wash your pet with the mixture. The solution cuts the greasy skunk spray and gets rid of the odor. Do not get mixture into eyes. Use any leftover mixture to wash areas or towels that have spray on them, but do not store the remainder. Baking soda and peroxide form a gas that can break a tightly sealed container.

SNAKES

~ Keep vegetation short around the house. Place gravel near your foundation if snakes are a problem there.

~ Keep rodent populations down. If the snakes have nothing to eat, they will move on.

~ Snakes like to hide under objects, so raise woodpiles or trash cans at least ten inches off the ground. Remove rock piles, too.

~ Place hardware cloth over drains and cracks around your house and outbuilding foundations.

TREE SQUIRRELS

~ To keep squirrels from climbing certain trees, make sure there are no limbs from other trees that lead to the tree, and place a twenty-four-inch metal band six to eight feet up the trunk.

~ To keep squirrels from digging up bulbs, place a piece of chicken wire over the bed until the bulbs sprout.

~ Sticky stuff, such as Tanglefoot, placed as a barrier works well to deter squirrels.

Glossary

abdomen—the posterior portion of the body.

acid soil—soil with a pH reading below 7. Can also be called *sour* soil.

aeration—a mechanical process that either punches holes or breaks up the soil to allow oxygen in and relieve the effects of soil compaction.

aerobic—anything that requires oxygen.

alkaline soil—soil with a pH reading above 7. Can also be called *sweet* soil.

amendment—a material that is added to soil to improve its condition or nutrient value.

annual—a plant that completes its life cycle in one growing season.

Bacillus thuringiensis—a bacterium known as Bt, it is the most widely used microbial biological control measure on the market today. There are more than thirty-five varieties, several of which are available to home gardeners. It is selective—only affecting the insects described on the label. It comes in many forms including liquid, powder, dust, and granules.

bacteria—microscopic organisms that can be parasitic or beneficial, and have round, rod, spiral, or filament-shaped cell bodies.

beneficial—a term used to describe a plant or animal that contributes to the well-being of people or nature.

beneficial insects—insects that control other harmful insects, or increase the productivity or fertility of plants.

biennial—a plant that requires two growing seasons to complete its life cycle.

biological control (biocontrol)—any living thing or biologically derived substance that controls or reduces the number of parasites, weeds, or other pests.

brassica—a member of the cabbage family of plants, which includes broccoli, cauliflower, brussels sprouts, collards, and kale.

broadcast—to scatter seeds or spread fertilizer evenly over a wide area.

broad-leafed plant—a plant that has a wide, flat leaf as opposed to the needlelike leaves of conifers.

bulb—a swollen underground stem where food is stored for the plant's period of dormancy.

calcareous—a term used to describe alkaline soils that contain limestone.

cane—a thin woody stem from such plants as bamboo and blackberries.

carnivore—an organism that feeds on the flesh of other organisms.

castings—worm manure or excrement.

caterpillar—the larval form of a butterfly or moth.

chemical control—to reduce the populations of pests by using chemical solutions.

chlorosis—a condition in plants that causes a loss of chlorophyll, generally caused by a lack of nutrients, especially iron. Characterized by yellowing foliage.

clay soil—a soil that is heavy with lots of clay particles in it. It is often easily compacted and slow-draining.

cold-blooded—describing an animal that has a body temperature that is regulated by its surroundings instead of its body.

compaction—the pressing together of soil particles, which in turn makes the soil hard.

companion planting—planting different plants together that are considered to have a beneficial effect on one another.

complete metamorphosis—complete change in form in the maturing process of certain insects, which involves four stages: egg, larva, pupa, adult.

composite flower—members of the daisy or composite family that have many small flowers packed tightly together to form a single flower head.

compost—nutrient-rich organic matter that is created by the decomposition of plants and animal wastes. Often used as a soil amendment.

composting—the process that occurs when organic matter is broken down by decomposer organisms into a nutrient-rich soil or humus.

cross-pollinate—to apply pollen of a male flower to the stigma or female part of another flower.

cucurbit—a member of the gourd family, which includes squash, cucumbers, and melons.

cultivar—a name given to a plant that has been selected from the wild or garden and cultivated to preserve certain characteristics.

cutting—a leaf, shoot, root, stem, or bud that has been cut off a plant to be used for propagation.

deadheading—the removal of faded flowers to discourage the formation of seeds and encourage more blooming.

deciduous—nonevergreen trees and shrubs that lose their leaves at the end of their growing season and grow new ones at the start of their next growing season.

decomposers—organisms that digest and break down the organic matter in the dead bodies of animals and other plants into simpler compounds.

decomposition—the process of breaking down organic matter into its basic compounds and elements, including nutrients needed for plant growth.

dividing—the process of separating a plant in order to propagate more plants from it.

dolomitic limestone—a form of limestone that contains small amounts of magnesium.

dormancy—the period of time a plant rests.

dormant oil—an oil used to smother overwintering insects such as scales on plants and trees.

drench—the application of water with or without added ingredients to the roots of a plant.

earthworm—a segmented worm that belongs to the phylum *Annelida*.

evergreen—a plant that has leaves the entire year.

family—a group of plant or animal genera having overall similar characteristics.

fertilizer—a substance that is added to the soil to supply one or more plant nutrients; it can be either natural or man-made.

fish emulsion—a liquid fertilizer made from fish.

floating row cover—a lightweight fabric that is placed over planted rows as a protection against frost or pests.

food wastes—food scraps; generally refers to uncooked fruit and vegetable scraps.

friable soil—easily crumbled soil.

fungicide—substance used to kill or inhibit fungi growth.

gall—an abnormal growth on a plant that is caused by insects, mites, or fungi.

genus—a like group of plants or animals within a family that has one or more species. It is the first word in the scientific Latin name of a plant or animal.

germinate—to begin to grow or to sprout from seed.

glauconite—an iron potassium silicate present in greensand.

grafted root stock—roots from one plant that have been combined, or grafted, with the top part of another plant. Generally root stocks are used because the root system from the top plant has a problem or the root stock itself is superior in some way.

green manure—plants used or grown to produce fertilizers, such as nitrogen, for the soil.

greensand—a sediment composed of grains of glauconite mixed with clay or sand and used as an organic fertilizer.

grub—the larval form of some beetles.

guano—the dried droppings of birds or bats.

habitat—a place where an organism normally lives.

heap—an unenclosed compost pile.

herbicide—a substance used to kill weeds or other plants.

hibernation—dormancy during the winter.

honeydew—a sweet liquid that is secreted onto the leaves of plants by aphids and other insects.

humus—finished compost, which has undergone a high degree of decomposition through the breakdown of plant and animal matter. It is stable, dark in color, and has a high water absorption and swelling capability.

incomplete metamorphosis—a gradual change in form from egg to adult in some insects. The stages are called *molts*, and there is no caterpillar or pupal form: the insect goes from egg to nymph to adult.

integrated pest management (IPM)—a pest management strategy that examines all aspects of pest management and comes up with a comprehensive analysis of the problem, in order to produce the maximum crop yield and the minimum adverse effects to man and the environment.

larva—the immature stage between the egg and pupa in insects that undergo complete metamorphosis.

leaf litter—the uppermost organic materials that are partly or not at all decomposed, on the surface of the soil.

macroorganisms—organisms that can be seen without magnification.

maggot— a legless fly larva that does not have a well-developed head.

manure—a term that usually refers to animal dung but is also used to describe plants grown as fertilizers for other plants (*green manure*).

microorganisms—organisms that are extremely small and cannot be seen without magnification.

migrate—to move from one location to another for food or reproduction.

mulch—a layer of partially decomposed plant materials that is placed on top of garden beds and around plants and shrubs to hold in moisture. Some even repel pests.

nectar—a sweet liquid secreted by plants.

nematode—an unsegmented roundworm belonging to the phylum *Nematoda;* these worms have a straight digestive tract that lies loose within a fluid-filled body space.

nitrogen fixation—ability of plants or other organisms to convert nitrogen from the air into a biologically usable form.

nymph—a stage in incomplete metamorphosis. Nymphs are immature insects that resemble tiny adults.

organic matter—any organic material derived from plants or animals that is in a more or less advanced stage of decomposition.

overwinter—the ability to live through or survive the winter.

parasite—an animal or plant that lives in or on the body of another living organism (host) for at least part of its life.

pest—an organism (either insect or animal) that is either harmful or annoying to humans or plants.

pesticide—a chemical used to control or kill pests, most commonly insect pests.

pH—the degree of alkalinity or acidity; it is measured numerically on a scale from 0 to 14.

pheromone—a substance produced by one organism that influences the behavior or physiology of another organism of the same species.

pheromone traps—artificial scent lures that imitate the sex attractant hormones of a certain insect species.

plant hormones—specific chemicals produced by plants that control certain growth aspects like flowering. Also called *growth regulators*.

proboscis—an extended mouthpart, which in insects can be beaklike or tubelike. Adult butterflies have a proboscis.

pupa—the stage between the larva and the adult form in insects with complete metamorphosis. This stage is nonfeeding and inactive.

rhizome—a below-ground-level stem that is capable of producing a new plant.

scarification—the process of nicking or chemically inducing a hard seed coat to open for quicker germination.

soil—an ecological system consisting of inorganic minerals, organic matter, and living organisms.

species—a group of individuals that are similar in structure and physiology and when mated are capable of reproducing fertile offspring.

stolon—a stem that runs along the ground in some plants, such as Bermuda grass, that forms roots and new plants at intervals along its length.

stomata—pores on the underside of leaves that gases can easily move through.

stratification—to expose seeds to cold to improve or speed germination.

thatch—a layer of organic material that develops between the soil and the base of plants. Often associated with lawn clippings that are matted on the soil surface, as well as shallow roots.

thorax—the body region in insects between the head and the abdomen; it has the walking legs and the wings.

true bugs—insects in the order *Hemiptera*. They have beaks or piercing mouthparts, wings that are thick at the base and membranous at the ends, and a metathorax that forms a triangular plate between the wing bases. Some examples of true bugs are stink bugs, assassin bugs, and waterboatmen.

vermicompost—the end product from composting with worms. Vermicompost contains worm castings, broken-down organic matter, bedding, worm cocoons, worms, and other organisms.

warm-blooded—describing an animal that has its body temperature regulated from within its body.

wilt—the discoloration and usually drooping of leaves caused by either excessively dry or excessively wet conditions.

Bibliography

Books and Magazines

Arkin, Frieda. *The Essential Kitchen Gardener.* New York: Henry Holt, 1991.

Ball, Jeff, and Liz Ball. *Landscape Problem Solver.* Emmaus, PA: Rodale Press, 1989.

Benjamin, Joan, and Deborah L. Martin (Eds.). *Great Garden Shortcuts.* Emmaus, PA: Rodale Press, 1996.

Bernstein, Chuck. *The Joy of Birding.* Santa Barbara, CA: Capra Press, 1984.

Boror, Donald J., and Richard E. White. *A Field Guide to Insects.* New York: Houghton Mifflin, 1970.

Buchanan, Rita, and Roger Holmes (Eds.). *Taylor's Master Guide to Gardening.* New York: Houghton Mifflin, 1994.

Dole, Claire Hagen. "Butterfly Gardens." *Country Living*, July 1999, pp. 32–34.

Ellis, Barbara. *Attracting Birds & Butterflies.* New York: Houghton Mifflin, 1997.

Ellis, Barbara, and Fern Marshall Bradley (Eds.). *The Organic Gardener's Handbook of Natural Insect and Disease Control.* Emmaus, PA: Rodale Press, 1996.

Farrand, John, Jr. (Ed.). *The Audubon Society Master Guide to Birding.* New York: Alfred A. Knopf, 1983.

Faulkner, Meryl A. *Project Wildlife—Injured and Orphaned Wildlife.* San Diego, CA: Project Wildlife, 1987.

Gallerstein, Gary A. *Bird Owner's Home Health and Care Handbook.* New York: Howell Book House, 1985.

Garden Pests & Diseases. Menlo Park, CA: Sunset Publishing, 1993.

Garrett, J. Howard. *Organic Manual.* Fort Worth, TX: Summit Group, 1993.

Grainger, Janette, and Connie Moore. *Natural Insect Repellents.* Austin, TX: Herb Bar, 1991.

Harrison, George H. *Garden Birds of America.* Minocqua, WI: Willow Creek Press, 1996.

Holmes, Roger (Ed.). *Taylor's Guide to Natural Gardening*. New York: Houghton Mifflin, 1993.

Johnsgard, Paul A. *The Hummingbirds of North America*. Washington, DC: Smithsonian Institution Press, 1983.

Lawns & Ground Covers. Menlo Park, CA: Sunset Publishing, 1979.

McGrath, Mike (Ed.). *The Best of Organic Gardening*. Emmaus, PA: Rodale Press, 1996.

Milne, Lorus, Margery Milne, and Susan Rayfield. *Audubon Society Field Guide to North American Insects and Spiders*. New York: Alfred A. Knopf, 1980.

Nancarrow, Loren, and Janet Hogan Taylor. *Dead Snails Leave No Trails*. Berkeley, CA: Ten Speed Press, 1996.

Nancarrow, Loren, and Janet Hogan Taylor. *The Worm Book*. Berkeley, CA: Ten Speed Press, 1998.

New Western Garden Book. Menlo Park, CA: Sunset Publishing Co., 1979.

Opler, Paul A., and Vichai Malidul. *Peterson Field Guides: Eastern Butterflies*. New York: Houghton Mifflin, 1992.

Opler, Paul A., and Amy Bartlett Wright. *Peterson Field Guides: Western Butterflies*. New York: Houghton Mifflin, 1999.

Orr, Robert T. *Vertebrate Biology*. Philadelphia: W.B. Saunders, 1971.

Pleasant, Barbara. *The Gardener's Bug Book*. Pownal, VT: Storey Communications, 1994.

Sachs, Paul. *Healthy Grass, Safe Lawn Organic Gardening*, May/June 1999, pp. 46–51.

Schneck, Marcus. *The Bird Feeder*. New York: Barnes and Noble Books, 1995.

Seidenberg, Charlotte. *The Wildlife Garden*. Jackson, MS: University Press, 1995.

Simpson, Daniel. "Precious Pollinators." *Zoonooz*, May 1999, pp. 27–31.

Songbirds, All the World's Animals. New York: Torstar Books, 1985.

Tekulsky, Mathew. *Butterfly Garden*. Boston: Harvard Common Press, 1985.

Turner, Brian. *Butterflies and Moths*. Secaucus, NJ: Chartwell Books, 1977.

Warton, Susan (Ed.). *Attracting Birds*. Menlo Park, CA: Sunset Publishing, 1994.

Wilson, Lois. *The Complete Gardener*. New York: Hawthorn Books, 1972.

Internet Resources

The Butterfly Conservancy
www.butterflywings.com/garden.html

Butterfly Gardening and Conservation, Missouri Department of
Conservation
www.conservation.state.mo.us/nathis/insects/butterf/butterf.html

Butterfly Guide
www.butterflies.com/guide.html

The Butterfly Website
www.butterflywebsite.com/index.htm

Electronic Resources on Lepidoptera
www.chebucto.ns.ca/Environment/NHR/lepidoptera.html

Gardening Naturally, *The Natural Gardener*
www.bbg.org/gardening/natural/bird/intro.html

The Hummingbird Society
www.hummingbird.org/hummer.htm

Michigan State University Extension
www.msue.msu.edu/vanburen/trapsweb.htm

National Bird-Feeding Society
www.birdfeeding.org

The National Wildlife Federation
www.nwf.org/habitats/backyard/basics.cfm

North Dakota State University Extension Service
www.ag.ndsu.nodak.edu

University of Arizona
http://insected.arizona.edu/bflyrear.htm

University of Illinois Extension, *Horticulture Solutions Series*
www.ag.uiuc.edu/~robsond/solutions/horticulture/docs/ironchlr.html

University of Minnesota, *Butterfly Gardening,* by Vera Krischik
www.ent.agri.umn.edu/cures/extpubs/6711/DG6711a.html

Buying Guide

EARTHWORMS
Williams Worm Farm
Cyclone Manufacturing
14893 El Monte Road
Lakeside, CA 92040
Tel: (619) 443-1698
Worms, worm bins, castings, worm
    tea, and supplies

INSECT CONTROLS AND TRAPS
Agro-BioTech
P.O. Box 2622
Woodinville, WA 98072
Tel: (425) 487-6011
Website: www.halcyon.com/
    agrobio.yellbluepage.htm

Gardener's Supply Co.
128 Intervale Road
Burlington, VT 05401
Tel: (802) 863-1700
Fax: (802) 660-4600

Insects Limited
10540 Jessup Boulevard
Indianapolis, IN 46280
Tel: (317) 846-3399

Olson Products
P.O. Box 103
Medina, OH 44258
Tel: (216) 723-3210

PCS—Pest Control Suppliers
4965 Jackson Street
Denver, CO 80216-3712
Tel: (800) 434-5893
Website: www.pcspest.com

SEED COMPANIES
W. Atlee Burpee & Company
300 Park Avenue
Warminster, PA 18991-0001
Tel: (800) 888-1447
Fax: (800) 487-5530
Website: http://garden.burpee.com

Gurney's Seed & Nursery Co.
110 Capital Street
Yankton, SD 57079
Tel: (605) 665-1930
Fax: (605) 665-9710

Johnny's Selected Seeds
310 Foss Hill Road
Albion, ME 04910
Tel: (207) 437-4301
Fax: (800) 437-4290
E-mail: homegarden@johnnyseeds.
    com
Website: www.johnnyseeds.com
Green manure seeds

Peaceful Valley Farm Supply Co.
P.O. Box 2209
Grass Valley, CA 95945
Green manure seeds, nursery stock

Pinetree Garden Seeds
Box 300
New Gloucester, ME 04260
Tel: (888) 527-3337
Fax: (207) 926-3886
E-mail:
    superseeds@worldnet.att.net
Green manure seeds, garden seeds

Seeds of Change
P.O. Box 15700
Santa Fe, NM 87506-5700
Tel: (888) 762-7333
Fax: (888) 329-4762
Website: www.seedsofchange.com
Seeds, tools, books, catalog

Shepherd's Garden Seeds
30 Irene Street
Torrington, CT 06790

Wildflower Carpet, Inc.
1325 S. Colorado Boulevard
Suite 404
Denver, CO 80222
Tel: (800) 247-6945

ORGANIC GROWERS AND SUPPLIERS

Biosys
1057 E. Meadow Circle
Palo Alto, CA 94303
Tel: (415) 856-9500
Organic products

Gardens Alive
5100 Schenley Place
Lawrenceburg, IN 47025
Tel: (812) 537-8650
Fax: (812) 537-5108
Catalog

Grangettos Farm and Garden
Supply
1105 W. Mission Avenue
Escondido, CA 92025
Tel: (760) 745-4671
Organic products, free catalog

Harmony Farm Supply
P.O. Box 460
Grafton, CA 95444
Tel: (707) 823-9125
Fax: (707) 823-1734

High Country Gardens
2902 Rufina Street
Santa Fe, NM 87505-2929
Tel: (800) 925-9387
Fax: (800) 925-0097
Catalog

Mellinger's Nursery
2310 W. South Range Road
North Lima, OH 44452
Tel: (800) 321-7444
Organic fertilizers, pesticides, seeds,
    beneficial insects

Nature's Control
P.O. Box 35
Medford, OR 97501
Tel: (503) 899 8318

Necessary Trading Company
P.O. Box 603
New Castle, VA 24127
Organic farming products, catalog

The Orchard
Route 2, Box 22 A
Rockwall, TX 75087
Tel: (214) 771-2097
Organic orchard supplies

Simpson's Nursery
13925 Highway 94
Jamul, CA 91935
Organic products

Walter Andersen's Nursery
3642 Enterprise
San Diego, CA 92110-3212
Tel: (619) 224-8271
Various organic products

Whatever Works
Earth Science Building
74 20th Street
Brooklyn, NY 11232
Tel: (800) 499-6757
Organic pest control products,
catalog

SOIL TESTING

Cook's Consulting
R.D. 2, Box 13
Lowville, NY 13367
Tel: (315) 376-3002

Peaceful Valley Farm Supply
P.O. Box 2209
Grass Valley, CA 95945
Tel: (916) 272-4769
Fax: (916) 272-4794
Basic soil test, test for micro-
nutrients, organic
recommendations

Timberleaf Soil Testing Services
39648 Old Spring Road
Murrieta, CA 92563
Tel: (909) 677-7510
Complete soil tests for basic and
trace minerals, organic
recommendations included

Wallace Laboratories
365 Coral Circle
El Segundo, CA 90245
Tel: (310) 615-0116
Fax: (310) 640-6863
Tests for soil fertility, essential
nutrients, toxic heavy metals,
recommendations provided

Woods End Research Laboratory
P.O. Box 297
Mt. Vernon, ME 04352
Tel: (207) 293-2457
Fax: (207) 293-2488
Soil testing for compost and soil,
offers compost testing kit

BENEFICIAL INSECTS

*Note: Before purchasing any organism,
consult the supplier or your local
agriculture department regarding any
restrictions in your area.*

American Insectaries, Inc.
30805 Rodriguez Road
Escondido, CA 92026-5312
Tel: (760) 751-1436
Fax: (760) 749-7061
Retail, wholesale, insects and mites

The Beneficial Insect Company
244 Forrest Street
Fort Mill, SC 29715
Tel: (803) 547-2301
Retail, wholesale, catalog

Beneficial Resources Inc.
P.O. Box 327
Danville, PA 17821
Tel: (800) 268-4377
Fax: (717) 271-1187
Retail, wholesale

Bio AG Supply
710 South Columbia
Plainview, TX 79072
Tel: (800) 746-9900
Fax: (806) 293-0712
Retail, wholesale, consulting, food
for beneficials, price list

Bio-Agronomics
P.O. 1013
Clovis, CA 93613
Tel: (209) 297-9288
Retail, wholesale, consulting

M&R Durango, Inc. Insectary
P.O. Box 886
Bayfield, CO 81122
Tel: (970) 259-3521
Fax: (970) 259-3857
Retail, wholesale, free brochure,
    consulting

Sierra Ag
2749 E. Malaga Avenue
Fresno, CA 93726
Tel: (559) 233-0585
Fax: (559) 237-0633
E-mail: IPM@sierraag.com
Website: www.sierraag.com
Retail, wholesale, insect traps

Insects for School Projects
Berkshire Biological
264 Main Road
Westhampton, MA 01027
Tel: (413) 527-3932
Fax: (413) 529-9382
Website: www.berkshirebio.com
Insects, butterflies, and other
    organisms

Organizations

BUTTERFLIES

Butterfly Lovers International
210 Columbus Avenue
San Francisco, CA 94133
Newsletter, journal

The Lepidopterists' Society
Michael J. Smith, Membership
1608 Presido Way
Roseville, CA 95661
Website: www.furman.edu/~
synder/synder/lep/index.html
Newsletter and journal

Monarch Watch
Department of Entomology
University of Kansas
Lawrence, KS 66045
Tel: 1-888-TAGGING
Monarch tracking, classroom
program, raising monarchs,
mailing list

**North American Butterfly
Association**
4 Delaware Road
Morristown, NJ 07960
Tel: (973) 285-0907
Fax: (973) 285-0936
E-mail: maba@naba.org
Website: www.naba.org
Magazine and two newsletters,
July 4 butterfly counts

The Xerces Society
4828 Southeast Hawthorne
Boulevard
Portland, OR 97215
Tel: (503) 232-6639
Website: www.xerces.org
Magazine and butterfly count

Young Entomologists' Society
1915 Peggy Place
Lansing, MI 48910-2553
Newsletter and trading,
$10.00/year

PLANTS AND GARDENING

American Begonia Society
157 Monument Road
Rio Dell, CA 95562-1617
Website: www.begonias.org

American Bonsai Society
P.O. Box 1136
Puyallup, WA 98374-1136
Tel: (206) 841-8992
Website: www.bonsai.org/abs
_home.html

American Camellia Society
Massee Lane Gardens
One Massee Lane
Fort Valley, GA 31030
Tel: (912) 967-2722
Fax: (912) 967-2083
Website: www.peach.public.lib.
ga.us/ACS/intro.htm

**American Community Gardening
Association**
c/o The Pennsylvania Horticulture
Society
100 N. 20th Street, 5th floor
Philadelphia, PA 19103-1495
Tel: (215) 988-8785
E-mail: sallymcc@libertynet.org
Website:
http://communitygarden.org
Bimonthy newsletter, training
programs

American Conifer Society
P.O. 360
Keswick, VA 22947-0360
Tel. & Fax: (804) 984-3660
E-mail: ACSconifer@aol.com
Web site. www.pacificrim.net/~
bydesign/acs3.htm

American Daffodil Society
Regional societies throughout
United States
Pacific—Nancy Tachett,
Membership
066 Green Street
Martinez, CA 94553
Tel: (925) 372-8083
E-mail: nancyt@netvista.net
Eastern—Elizabeth Ellwood
12 Auldwood Lane
Rumson, NJ 07760
Tel: (908) 842-7945
E-mail: Sallyprune@aol.com
Website: www.mc.edu/~adswww

The American Dahlia Society
16816 County Road 10
Bristol, IN 46507
Tel: (219) 848-4888
Website: http://sashimi.wwa.com
/~jjf/ads.html

American Dianthus Society
P.O. Box 22232
Santa Fe, NM 87502-22232
Tel: (505) 438-7038
E-mail: randbear@nets.com

American Fern Society
Dr. David Lellinger (Membership
Secretary)
326 West Street NW
Vienna, VA 22180-4151
Website: www.visuallink.net/fern
/index.html
Journal, information

American Fuchsia Society
Judy Salome, Membership
6979 Clark Road
Paradise, CA 95659-2210
E-mail: ejsalome@aol.com
Website: www.slip.net/~afs

American Horticultural Society at
River Farm
7931 E. Boulevard Drive
Alexandria, VA 22308-9801
Tel: (703) 768-5700
Fax: (703) 768-8700
Website: www.ahs.org
Publications

American Iris Society
Marilyn Harlow, Dept. E,
Membership Secretary
P.O. Box 8455
San Jose, CA 95155-8455
Tel: (408) 971-0444
E-mail: Marilyn Harlow at
103262.1512@compuserve.com
Website: www.irises.org

American Orchid Society
6000 South Olive Avenue
W. Palm Beach, FL 33405
Tel: (407) 585-8666
Fax: (407) 585-0654
Website: orchidweb.org
Magazine

American Rhododendron Society
11 Pinecrest Drive
Fortuna, CA 95540
Tel: (707) 725-3043
Fax: (707) 725-1217
Website: www.rhododendron.org
Quarterly journal

American Rose Society
P.O. Box 30,000
Shreveport LA 71130-0030

Tel: (318) 938-5402
Fax: (318) 938-5405
E-mail: ars@ars-hq.org
Website: www.ars.org

Azalea Society of America
Several regional chapters
Brookside Garden Chapter
Bill Miller
7613 Quintana Court
Bethesda, MD 20817
Tel: (301) 365-0692
Website: www.theazaleaworks.
    com/asa.htm
Publications

Cactus and Succulent Society of American
Mindy Fusaro, Treasurer,
    Membership
P.O. Box 2615
Pahrump, NV 89041-2615
Tel: (775) 751-1357
Website: www.cactus-
    mall.com/essa/index.html

Garlic Seed Foundation
Rose Valley Farm
Rose, NY 14542-0419
Tel: (315) 587-9787

Herb Society of America
9010 Kirtland Chardon Road
Kirtland, OH 44094
Tel: (216) 256-0541
Website: www.ats.edu/faculty/
    spons/H0000383.HTM

International Carnivorous Plant Society
PMB 330
3310 East Yorba Linda Boulevard
Fullerton, CA 92831-1709
Website: www.carnivorousplants.
    org/us.htm
Newsletter

International Geranium Society
P.O. Box 92734
Pasadena, CA 91109-2734
Tel: (818) 908-8867 (West Coast)
or (405) 472-4203 (East Coast)
Website: www.geocities.com/
    RainForest/2822
Newsletter

The Lady Bird Johnson Wildflower Center
4801 La Crosse Avenue
Austin, TX 87839
Tel: (512) 292-4100
E-mail: nwrc@onr.com
Website: www.wildflower.org

North American Lily Society
P.O. Box 272
Owatonna, MN 55060-0272
Tel: (507) 451-2170
Website: www.oxford.net/~lilium
    /nals/index.html
Quarterly bulletin and yearbook

WILDLIFE

American Birding Association
P.O. Box 6599
Colorado Springs, CO 80934
Tel: (800) 850-2473
Website: www.americanbirding.
    org/eventfestgen.htm
Newsletter, magazine, books,
    birding equipment

Cornell Lab of Ornithology
159 Sapsucker Woods Road
Ithaca, NY 14850
Tel: (607) 254-2446
Citizen-Science projects, Project
    Feeder Watch, Box Network,
    Project Pigeon Watch, House
    Finch Disease Survey, and
    Birdscope newsletter

Defenders of Wildlife
1101 14th Street, N.W. #1400
Washington, DC 20005
Tel: (202) 682-9400
Website:
www.defenders.org/index.html
Magazine, newsletters, Habitat
Bears (Florida), Watchable
Wildlife program, state viewing
guides

Florida Panther Society
Route 1, Box 1895
White Springs, FL 32096
Tel: (904) 397-2945
Website: www.atlantic.net/~
oldfla/panther/panther.html
Newsletter and panther adoption

National Audubon Society
P.O. Box 52529
Boulder, CO 80322-2529
Website: www.birder.com
Christmas bird count, Project
Feederwatch, Adopt-a-Bird,
outings, magazine, discounts,
and Living Oceans programs

National Wildlife Federation
8925 Leesburg Pike
Vienna, VA 22184
Tel: (703) 791-4000
Website: www.nwf.org
Urban Wildlife and Backyard
Habitat programs, magazine

The Nature Conservancy
222 S. Westmore Drive, Ste. 300
Altamonte Springs, FL 32714
Tel: (407) 682-3664
Website: www.tnc.org
Habitat protection, bimonthly
magazine, newsletters, field
trips, activities, Adopt-an-Acre,
and Rescue the Reef

North American Bluebird Society
P.O. Box 74 Department P
Darlington, WI 53530
Website:
www.nabluebirdsociety.org
Transcontinental Bluebird Trail
Project

Save the Manatee Club
500 N. Maitland Avenue
Maitland, FL 32751
Tel: (800) 432-JOIN
E-mail:
education@savethemanatee.org
Website: www.savethemanatee.org
Adopt-a-Manatee, information,
gifts, and action alerts

Sea Turtle League
4424 N.W. 13th Street, Suite #A1
Gainesville, FL 32609
Tel: (800) 678-7853
E-mail: ccc@cccturtle.org
Website: www.cccturtle.org
Adopt-a-Turtle, quarterly
newsletter, turtle tracking via
the web, and action alerts

Sierra Club
85 Second Street, Second Floor
San Francisco, CA 94105-3441
Tel: (415) 977-5500
Fax: (415) 977-5799
E-mail: information@sierraclub.org
Website: www.sierraclub.org
Magazine, discounts, and outings

World Wildlife Fund
1250 24th Street
Washington DC 20037
Tel: (800) 225-5993
Website: www.wwf.org

Index